WHEN & HOW
TO USE MENTAL HEALTH RESOURCES

SECOND EDITION

ALSO BY KENNETH C. HAUGK

Christian Caregiving—a Way of Life

Speaking the Truth in Love: How to Be an Assertive Christian (with Ruth N. Koch)

Don't Sing Songs to a Heavy Heart: How to Relate to Those Who Are Suffering

Antagonists in the Church: How to Identify and Deal with Destructive Conflict

Antagonists in the Church Study Guide (with Amity V. Haugk)

Caring for Inactive Members: How to Make God's House a Home

Reopening the Back Door: Answers to Questions about Ministering to Inactive Members

Discovering God's Vision for Your Life: You and Your Spiritual Gifts

Journeying through Grief:

- *A Time to Grieve*
- *Experiencing Grief*
- *Finding Hope and Healing*
- *Rebuilding and Remembering*

The Quest for Quality Caring

Leader Killers: How to Identify and Deal with Antagonists in Your Organization

Cancer—Now What? Taking Action, Finding Hope, and Navigating the Journey Ahead

WHEN & HOW TO USE MENTAL HEALTH RESOURCES

SECOND EDITION

KENNETH C. HAUGK, Ph.D.
ISAAC B. AKERS

STEPHEN MINISTRIES • ST. LOUIS, MISSOURI

WHEN AND HOW TO USE MENTAL HEALTH RESOURCES: A STEPHEN MINISTRY GUIDE

Copyright © 2000, 2020 by Stephen Ministries St. Louis. All rights reserved.

ISBN: 978-1-930445-07-9

Library of Congress Catalog Card Number: 2019952764

Scripture quotations, unless otherwise noted, are taken from the Holy Bible, NEW INTERNATIONAL VERSION®, NIV® Copyright © 1973, 1978, 1984, 2011 by Biblica, Inc.® Used by permission. All rights reserved worldwide.

No portion of this publication may be reproduced, stored in a retrieval system, or transmitted in any form or by any means—whether electronic, mechanical, photocopying, recording, or otherwise—except for brief quotations in articles or reviews, without the prior written permission of the publisher. For permission, write to:

Stephen Ministries Permissions Department
2045 Innerbelt Business Center Drive
St. Louis, Missouri 63114-5765

Printed in the U.S.A.

20
1

This book is dedicated to all those who provide care—Stephen Ministers, Stephen Leaders, pastors, mental health professionals, and others—and to those who receive care, that they may have full health in body, mind, and spirit

CONTENTS

Preface 1

1. The Purpose of This Book 5
2. Defining the Stephen Minister's Role 15
3. What Stephen Ministers Do 27
4. What Stephen Ministers Do Not Do 39
5. Stephen Ministry and Mental Health Professionals 51
6. When to Refer a Care Receiver to a
   Mental Health Professional 65
7. How to Refer a Care Receiver to a
   Mental Health Professional 79
8. After a Referral to a Mental Health Professional
   Has Been Made 99
9. Some Final Thoughts on Stephen Ministry
   and Mental Health Care 113

Appendix A: What to Say—and What Not to Say—When Referring a Care Receiver to a Mental Health Professional 123

Appendix B: Key Information for Mental Health Professionals to Know about Stephen Ministry 137

Appendix C: Guidelines for Mental Health Professionals Serving as Stephen Ministers 143

Notes 153

Acknowledgments 157

About the Authors 159

PREFACE

When I started Stephen Ministry in 1975, one of my goals was to create a ministry that drew on the best of both Christian and clinical caregiving practices, blending solid theological principles with sound psychology. With my training and experience as a pastor and a clinical psychologist, I valued the strengths of each approach and believed they could be used together to equip laypeople to provide high-quality, distinctively Christian care. For decades now, Stephen Leaders and Stephen Ministers have been doing just that, so I consider the idea a success.

One of the reasons that Stephen Ministry has worked so well over the years is a firm commitment to maintaining clear boundaries. Stephen Ministers, although well-trained and committed lay caregivers, are not equipped to deal with every need a care receiver may have—especially in the area of mental health. When such needs arise, a trained mental health professional should be brought into the situation to ensure that a hurting person receives the appropriate type and level of care for his or her needs. In this way, professional and lay caring can effectively complement each other in pursuit of the best outcome for those who are hurting.

Throughout my professional life, I have seen the valuable help that mental health professionals can offer to individuals who are struggling with depression, anxiety, and other issues that leave them less able to cope with life's challenges. The training these professionals go through, the expertise they offer, and their compassion for people who suffer from mental health issues can make a significant difference for those they serve. For these reasons and many more besides, mental health professionals can be a great asset to Stephen Ministry.

Over the years, I have heard many stories from Stephen Ministers and Stephen Leaders about the benefits care receivers have experienced after being referred to a mental health professional. One Stephen Minister told me about how he referred a care receiver who was struggling with long-term anger issues:

> "It became clear after a while that the issue was serious, so I talked with my Stephen Leaders and then suggested to my care receiver that he might want to talk to a counselor. After going to a few sessions just to try it out, he decided sticking with it was a priority for him. And it turned out just phenomenally—he eventually overcame those issues and experienced growth that transformed his whole life. It was amazing to see."

Another Stephen Minister shared how seeing a mental health professional helped her care receiver work through severe depression:

> "Six months after she started seeing a mental health professional, it was like night and day. She started seeing friends again, her outlook on life was more positive, and the light was back in her eyes. Her

receiving professional care helped me as a Stephen Minister, too, because it lifted a heavy weight that I couldn't carry on my own."

These are just two examples of how the care of a mental health professional—sometimes in tandem with that of a Stephen Minister—can make a profound difference in a person's life.

For a variety of reasons, people are sometimes anxious or uneasy about the possibility of relating to individuals who are dealing with mental health issues. As a Stephen Minister, though, you will be well prepared by your training to respond to situations involving the mental health of your care receiver. In particular, the material in this book will equip you with the knowledge and practical steps to take should a care receiver ever need to be referred to a mental health professional, preparing you for this important part of your ministry and serving as a reliable reference. This book is grounded in years of experience of Stephen Ministers and Stephen Leaders from congregations around the world, as well as careful research and review with mental health professionals to ensure its quality, accuracy, and effectiveness. You will see insights and thoughts shared by many of those individuals throughout.

Also know that you will not be on your own in any caring relationship. Your fellow Stephen Ministers in your Supervision Group and your Stephen Leaders will be there to support you. Most importantly, Christ will be caring for your care receiver through you, and God will strengthen you to provide the best possible care—including when this involves connecting a care receiver with professional help.

May God bless the care you offer to each care receiver you serve, including when you encounter those who struggle with mental health issues. I pray that this book will guide you in your caregiving—and that you will know that the Great Curegiver walks alongside you always.

Kenneth C. Haugk

THE PURPOSE OF THIS BOOK

The ultimate goal of Stephen Ministry is for hurting people to receive the best care possible. This is the reason Stephen Ministry exists and the purpose every Stephen Minister and Stephen Leader is dedicated to accomplishing. Stephen Leaders match people going through difficult times in life with Stephen Ministers, who then come alongside these individuals to offer high-quality, Christ-centered care. In the midst of suffering, what people need is a genuine, empathetic presence—not fix-it solutions, half-measures, or care at arm's length. Stephen Ministers understand this and seek to meet that need by striving to provide the best care they possibly can.

The most appropriate type and level of care, though, may not always be the care of a Stephen Minister. In a Stephen Ministry caring relationship, a care receiver's needs may change or develop beyond what Stephen Ministers, as lay caregivers, are trained to handle. In their training, Stephen Ministers learn the limitations of their caregiving and how to recognize when a care receiver needs to be connected with other kinds of help. When this happens, Stephen Ministers work together with their Stephen Leaders to find qualified individuals or organizations—such as mental health professionals or other community resources—who can provide the care best suited to the care receiver's needs. In short, if Stephen Ministers are not able to supply the care a care receiver needs, they help connect the person with a resource that can.

Connecting hurting people with support other than that of a Stephen Minister is consistent with the goal of Stephen Ministry—it's a matter of making sure care receivers receive the best possible care. Just as a family doctor might refer a patient to a surgeon for a specific procedure, so do Stephen Ministers on occasion need to rely on others, particularly professionals, to help address specific needs a care receiver may have.

One particular area where people often have needs for care beyond the scope of Stephen Ministry is that of mental health. Stephen Ministers serve people who face a wide range of challenges—personal crises, life transitions, overwhelming circumstances—any of which can affect a person's mental health. While the emotional and spiritual support Stephen Ministers provide often has positive benefits for care receivers' overall mental health, there are situations where the most appropriate type of care is that of a mental health professional. Connecting a care receiver with a mental health professional in these circumstances, then, is the way Stephen Ministers can best serve the goal of Stephen Ministry.

What Is This Book's Purpose?

The purpose of this book is:

> To equip Stephen Ministers with the knowledge and skills they need to appropriately use mental health resources to support their care receivers.

The book provides Stephen Ministers with a foundational understanding of their role as lay Christian caregivers and how that role relates to situations where a care receiver is experiencing mental health issues. It prepares Stephen Ministers to recognize signs that a care receiver may be experiencing mental health issues and know what steps to follow to ensure care receivers are connected with the proper care. It also shares guidelines and safeguards that help preserve the well-being of care receivers, Stephen Ministers, and a congregation's Stephen Ministry as a whole.

Although the specifics of professional mental health care vary between cities, states, and countries, the principles in this book are useful anywhere. Stephen Ministers who read this book can feel confident about handling situations involving the mental health of care receivers, and can rely on it as an ongoing reference throughout their ministry.

Whom Is This Book For?

This book is written primarily for Stephen Ministers. As caregivers who relate directly with care receivers, they are in a good position to notice signs that a care receiver may need professional help and initiate a process of referring a care receiver to the appropriate care. In addition, their strong caregiving skills make them great allies for people dealing with mental health issues; they possess the compassion, humility, and assertiveness to help people get the care they need.

A number of other groups can benefit from having a clear understanding of how Stephen Ministers function in the area of mental health. In particular, Stephen Leaders, pastors, and other church staff will find this knowledge useful as they work with their congregation's Stephen Ministry.

The Importance of Understanding the Stephen Minister's Role in Dealing with Mental Health Issues

When it comes to mental health issues, Stephen Ministers have a very specific role. Before getting into that role, though, it's necessary to define one key term—*mental disorder*—and what it means in the context of Stephen Ministry:

> A mental disorder is a syndrome characterized by clinically significant disturbance in an individual's cognition, emotion regulation, or behavior that reflects a dysfunction

in the psychological, biological, or developmental processes underlying mental functioning. Mental disorders are usually associated with significant distress or disability in social, occupational, or other important activities.[1]

In short, a mental disorder means that someone's ability to function in everyday life is hampered by some aspect of his or her mental state. As the phrase "clinically significant" indicates, it is also a specific psychological diagnosis. Because of this, Stephen Ministers do not diagnose care receivers with mental disorders. That is the realm of mental health professionals. However, Stephen Ministers can and should be aware of the signs of possible mental disorders. Stephen Ministers will not be assigned a care receiver who has a known mental disorder, but it's possible that a need for professional mental health care may arise during a caring relationship.

When identifying potential mental health issues in a care receiver, a Stephen Minister is not responsible for making a clinical assessment, but rather for noticing the signs and beginning a process of working with his or her Stephen Leaders to potentially refer the care receiver to a mental health professional. In this way, Stephen Ministers are like a ship's lookout, keeping their eyes on the horizon and alerting the key people as soon as they see any sign of trouble ahead. It's essential that Stephen Ministers understand and fulfill their role in this area in order to protect their care receivers, themselves, and their congregation's Stephen Ministry.

WHEN AND HOW TO USE MENTAL HEALTH RESOURCES

- Care receivers can be put at risk if a Stephen Minister tries to take sole responsibility for caring for someone struggling with mental health issues. If appropriate care is not offered to the care receiver, his or her well-being and safety can be compromised. Clearly, this would run counter to the goal of Stephen Ministry.

- Stephen Ministers are also likely to experience difficulties if they try to handle an inappropriate caring situation on their own. Because they are not equipped to deal with serious mental health issues, any attempt to do so can cause a host of problems, including stress, emotional exhaustion, compromised boundaries, feelings of inadequacy, and burnout. Overall, the Stephen Minister will be straining to provide a type and level of care beyond what he or she has been trained for.

- Finally, Stephen Ministry itself—as well as the congregation responsible for it—can be put at risk if a Stephen Minister does not refer a care receiver to the care of a mental health professional when needed. Issues within a congregation's Stephen Ministry could cause people's confidence in the ministry to be damaged, making it more difficult for it to continue.

These negative consequences can be avoided when Stephen Ministers understand the scope of their role as caregivers. Rather than attempting to provide care outside the boundaries of Stephen Ministry, they watch for the signs that a care receiver may have needs in those areas—and then assertively take the necessary steps to refer the care receiver to a mental health professional.

When Stephen Ministers diligently observe the boundaries of their role, care receivers can benefit greatly from being referred to the appropriate professional help. For a variety of reasons, including the social stigma often associated with mental health issues, people who are struggling with their mental health may be reluctant to reach out for help. Other care receivers may be willing to seek help but don't know where to turn. Still others may not have even thought of the possibility of receiving professional care. Whatever the situation, the involvement of a Stephen Minister can be an important source of encouragement and assistance for care receivers to take the first step toward getting the help they need.

Stephen Ministers Are Not Alone

Although Stephen Ministers meet with their care receivers one to one, a key principle they can draw confidence from is that they are not alone in their ministry; they have their Supervision Group and Stephen Leaders to rely on. As a clinical social worker and Stephen Minister said, "The structure of Stephen Ministry is designed to guide and encourage Stephen Ministers, starting with the foundation of supervision. Plus, they're also supported by their Stephen Leaders and pastor."

WHEN AND HOW TO USE MENTAL HEALTH RESOURCES

No Stephen Minister has to navigate the caring relationship and any potential challenges solo—nor should they. This is especially true when it comes to caring for care receivers who may be experiencing mental health issues. Because such situations carry the possibility of risk to the well-being of both the Stephen Minister and care receiver, it's essential that Stephen Ministers rely on this support to make sure care receivers get the appropriate kind of care.

Throughout this book, the term *refer* or *referral* is used to describe the overall process of connecting a care receiver with help outside of Stephen Ministry, including mental health professionals. Chapter 7, "How to Refer a Care Receiver to a Mental Health Professional," discusses this process in depth, the first step of which is getting consultation. Stephen Ministers always first talk with others before referring a care receiver to a mental health professional, and they continue to work alongside their Stephen Leaders until the care receiver has been successfully connected with professional care. So, whenever this book talks about Stephen Ministers *referring* care receivers to any kind of care outside Stephen Ministry, it means they're working the process of referring the care receiver with the guidance and assistance of others.

The fact that Stephen Ministers can look to their fellow Stephen Ministers, their Stephen Leaders, and their pastor for assistance in situations involving a care receiver's mental health contributes to their ministry in a significant way.

The Purpose of This Book

Not only does it help Stephen Ministers most effectively achieve the goal of care receivers getting the best possible care, but it also means that Stephen Ministers themselves receive vital support in their caregiving. There is no need for Stephen Ministers to take on sole responsibility for helping a care receiver who is experiencing mental health issues. Rather, they can rely on those who have also made a commitment to care for hurting people through Stephen Ministry. In situations involving mental health, as well as any other challenges they may encounter, Stephen Ministers can find comfort in this fact: They are not alone.

* * * * *

In the decades since Stephen Ministry was founded, thousands of care receivers have been connected with valuable professional mental health care thanks to Stephen Ministers and Stephen Leaders who recognized the signs of a need for professional mental health care, understood how to carry out their role, and assertively started the process of referring. As you read this book, you will be empowered to do the same—so that if a care receiver ever needs to be referred to a mental health professional, you will know what to do. In the process, you'll make a profound difference in the individual's life by helping ensure a hurting person receives the best care possible.

DEFINING THE STEPHEN MINISTER'S ROLE

Stephen Ministers occupy a unique and important space in caring ministry. As an extension of the pastor's care, they walk alongside people who are experiencing a wide range of life crises, serving as a valuable source of ongoing emotional and spiritual support for as long as care receivers need it. Additionally, they work within formal caring relationships that represent their commitment to their care receivers and to a high level of quality caring. Overall, Stephen Ministers are dedicated and qualified caregivers, capable of caring effectively for people with a wide variety of needs.

At the same time, Stephen Ministers do not function as pastors, counselors, or other professionals, even if a particular Stephen Minister happens to hold credentials in one of those fields. It's critical that Stephen Ministers understand the specific characteristics and boundaries of their role, as this knowledge helps them identify what kinds of care are and are not appropriate for them to provide—and then to communicate those boundaries to care receivers. By fully grasping the nature of their role, Stephen Ministers will be well equipped to navigate any areas of uncertainty they encounter during a caring relationship, including those involving care receivers' mental health.

A Closer Look at the Definition of a Stephen Minister

To get a complete picture of the Stephen Minister's role, it's helpful to start by considering the definition of a Stephen Minister.

> Stephen Ministers are lay Christian caregivers who are trained, commissioned, and supervised in their caring ministry.

The following sections discuss the elements of this definition.

Lay

Stephen Ministers are *lay* caregivers. They are not professionals, but volunteers who give of their gifts and time to serve hurting people. This fact establishes two clear boundaries around their role: Stephen Ministers do not provide any kind of professional care, and they do not accept payment for their ministry.

Along with these boundaries, Stephen Ministers' identity as laypeople also brings some unique advantages:

- Stephen Ministers are not bound by the same professional restrictions as professional caregivers, including mental health professionals. One licensed professional counselor who serves as a Stephen Minister shared, "Mental health professionals often have set, limited amounts of time to meet and work with clients. As Stephen Ministers, we also have boundaries, but we have more freedom to meet for a little longer, take a phone call when a care receiver is in crisis, or be flexible about where and when we meet."

- Stephen Ministers are free to initiate conversations about religious and spiritual topics. A social worker shared these thoughts: "What drew me to Stephen Ministry was the fact that, as a professional, I can't always say, 'What's your spiritual life like?' or 'Would you like to pray together?' Having the option to bring up God in the caring relationship is helpful for me, and it often helps my care receivers open up, too."

- The fact that Stephen Ministers do not accept payment for their ministry offers certain benefits, such as avoiding complications related to insurance.

Of course, none of these advantages is a reason to start or continue a Stephen Ministry caring relationship when a person needs professional help. For individuals whose needs are appropriate for Stephen Ministry, however, Stephen Ministers' status as lay caregivers can be a great benefit.

Christian

The distinctively *Christian* identity of Stephen Ministers is a foundational part of everything they are and do. At the root of their caregiving is the reality that Stephen Ministers are motivated to ministry by their faith in Christ and supported by the Holy Spirit in every caring relationship.

The Christian nature of Stephen Ministers is evident in a number of ways: their trust in God to bring results for their care receivers, their use of distinctively Christian caregiving tools, and how they relate to care receivers, fellow Stephen Ministers, and Stephen Leaders. It is also an expression of a profound truth of the Christian church—that every member of the body of Christ has been given gifts for building up the kingdom of God. As the Apostle Paul writes:

> There are different kinds of gifts, but the same Spirit distributes them. There are different kinds of service, but the same Lord. There are different kinds of working, but in all of them and in everyone it is the same God at work. Now to each one the manifestation of the Spirit is given for the common good. (1 Corinthians 12: 4–7)

Every Stephen Minister is different, but many have spiritual gifts of faith, mercy, teaching the faith, encouragement, and knowing.[1] As they care, Stephen Ministers live out their own God-given gifts in meaningful ministry.

Most importantly, being Christian means that Stephen Ministers bring more than just themselves to the caring relationship; they bring Christ with them, living out the Stephen Ministry motto, "Christ caring for people, through people." As Stephen Ministers care, they become tangible representations of God's love, presence, and comfort to their care receivers, which is more powerful than anything they could offer alone.

Caregivers

An essential part of the role of the Stephen Minister is being a *caregiver*. Stephen Ministers enter their caring relationships with the specific goal of serving the needs of the care receiver, not to have their own needs served. Stephen Ministry caring relationships are thus intentionally one-sided, focusing almost entirely on the care receiver and meeting his or her needs.

The word caregiver also speaks to a foundational part of the role: Stephen Ministers are there to give care rather than engage in other activities. Chapter 4, "What Stephen Ministers Do Not Do," covers the types of support outside the boundaries of Stephen Ministry, which include activities other than caregiving. Stephen Ministers do not allow those other activities to interfere with their caring relationship, always keeping in mind their purpose as caregivers—to walk alongside and support care receivers as they navigate difficult times in life.

Trained

Before they are assigned their first care receiver, Stephen Ministers are *trained* by Stephen Leaders in their congregation. To enter into the life of a person facing some life challenge—grief following the death of a loved one, the aftermath of a divorce, an unexpected medical crisis, or any number of other difficulties—is a sacred opportunity. As the book *Don't Sing Songs to a Heavy Heart* says, "When you offer care and comfort to another, you are stepping into a holy place, into the other person's unique universe of selfhood, need, and pain."[2] Stephen Ministers do not enter this holy place unprepared. They are thoroughly equipped with knowledge, skills, and tools that will allow them to provide high-quality care.

Preparing Christians for ministry has a strong biblical precedent. As recorded in Luke 10, Jesus himself trained the seventy-two before sending them out, giving specific instructions of what to take with them and what to do. Likewise, Stephen Minister training prepares Stephen Ministers to go out and care in ways that truly help their care receivers.

Commissioned

When Stephen Ministers finish their training, they are *commissioned* as a way to recognize and affirm their training for and commitment to ministry. Commissioning also formally establishes Stephen Ministers as representatives of their congregation, showing that the entire congregation stands behind them as they go out into the world to bring Christ's love to suffering people. With this commissioning comes the responsibility to represent their congregation and its mission well.

Supervised

Although Stephen Ministers meet individually with their care receivers, they aren't on their own in their ministry—each Stephen Minister is *supervised*. All Stephen Ministers participate in Supervision Groups, where they meet twice a month with their peers in ministry to receive and give support, guidance, and accountability. In addition, Stephen Leaders provide oversight of Stephen Ministry as a whole, including supervision and support of Stephen Ministers. Supervision in all its forms is a foundation Stephen Ministers can rely on, as well as a vital piece in maintaining the high quality of their care.

* * * * *

Together, these elements of the definition of a Stephen Minister form a picture of a unique kind of caregiver—one who understands the boundaries and advantages of being a lay caregiver, is grounded in the Christian faith, serves the care receiver's needs rather than his or her own, and is prepared for, supported during, and supervised in ministry.

Who Stephen Ministers Are Not

The definition of a Stephen Minister provides an understanding of who Stephen Ministers are, but it also clarifies who they are not. The following sections highlight a number of specific roles Stephen Ministers do not fulfill.

Stephen Ministers Are Not Therapists or Counselors

Although Stephen Ministers go through thorough training, they are still laypeople doing lay ministry, not professional caregivers. Therefore, Stephen Ministers are not accurately described by professional titles like *therapist* or *counselor*. While they use some of the same skills as therapists or counselors, such as active listening and helping care receivers process feelings, they do not make diagnoses and are not equipped to provide professional care, particularly when a person may be suffering from a mental disorder.

For this reason, congregations with Stephen Ministry are discouraged from referring to Stephen Ministers as *therapists* or *counselors*—or even as *lay therapists* or *lay counselors*. These titles can suggest that Stephen Ministers possess a level of expertise and qualification beyond what they've received in their training, which may be misleading to care receivers.

Stephen Ministers Are Not Pastors

While Stephen Ministers are extensions of the pastor's care and representatives of their congregations, they are not pastors themselves. Typically, pastoral training and formation is much more extensive than what Stephen Ministers experience, and it uniquely qualifies pastors for their role in congregational leadership. On the practical level of training and preparation, the distinction between Stephen Ministers and pastors is clear.

In addition, most Christian denominations make a distinction between the clergy and the laity in terms of their roles and responsibilities, and Stephen Ministers fall clearly into the category of the laity. This distinction is not to devalue the ministry of Stephen Ministers or laypeople in general; it just recognizes the reality that, as Paul writes, "We have different gifts, according to the grace given to each of us" (Romans 12:6). Pastors use their unique gifts and talents to fulfill a specific role and function in the congregation. The scope and nature of their ministry is largely different than that of Stephen Ministers, so it is not correct to label Stephen Ministers as *pastors* or *lay pastors*.

Stephen Ministers Are Not Spiritual Directors

Stephen Ministers often help care receivers deal with spiritual issues, but their role is different than that of a spiritual director even though many spiritual directors are laypeople themselves. There are, however, clear differences in training and purpose between the two. Typically, spiritual directors have gone through specialized training to prepare them for the role of guiding individuals in spiritual growth, with some denominations requiring individuals to earn certificates in spiritual direction before beginning to work with clients. Stephen Minister training has a different purpose and covers different content.

In addition, the focus of a caring relationship between a Stephen Minister and care receiver is on providing care in the midst of one or more life challenges. The relationship between spiritual director and directee, in contrast, is primarily oriented toward promoting personal spiritual growth.

Stephen Ministers Are Not Mutual Friends

A healthy Stephen Ministry caring relationship shares some characteristics with a friendship, but it's important that both Stephen Ministers and care receivers understand the differences between the two types of relationships. A friendship involves a mutual give-and-take, while in a Stephen Ministry caring relationship the Stephen Minister is specifically there to address the needs of the care receiver. The Stephen Minister's role in a care receiver's life is that of a caregiver, with the specific goal of providing care and addressing emotional and spiritual needs. Stephen Ministers are there to serve their care receivers, so the relationship is focused on helping the care receiver rather than being a mutual exchange.

As caregivers, Stephen Ministers also maintain boundaries that typically don't exist between friends. Module 7 of Stephen Minister training, "Maintaining Boundaries in Caregiving," lays out ways Stephen Ministers preserve the integrity of the caring relationship. In particular, appendix A of that module, "The Differences between a Friendship and a Stephen Ministry Caring Relationship," contains some helpful distinctions between these two roles.

This certainly doesn't mean that Stephen Ministers and care receivers cannot be friendly with each other. However, Stephen Ministers always need to keep in mind that their purpose is not to be the care receiver's friend but to provide the best possible care.

A Well-Defined Role Enables Effective Caring

One good way to understand where the Stephen Minister's role fits in with other kinds of caregivers is by looking at the Continuum of Care.

CONTINUUM OF CARE

Family and Friends	Small Groups	Stephen Ministers	Pastors	Mental Health Professionals
Informal care	Group support	One-to-one, ongoing, Christ-centered care and support	Pastoral care	Emotional & psychological care
		Filling an Important Gap		

◄──────────────── Level of Care Needed ────────────────►
Lower   Higher

This graphic illustrates that Stephen Ministers have an important role in caring for hurting people distinct from other kinds of caregivers. Just as the care of a close friend is different from the care offered by a therapist, so the care of Stephen Ministers is unique because of the specific characteristics that define their role.

Part of the reason Stephen Ministry is so effective is because the role of the Stephen Minister is so clearly defined. When Stephen Ministers know who they are and are not called to be, they are freed from unrealistic expectations or the need to handle situations they aren't equipped for. Most importantly, the well-defined role gives Stephen Ministers a firm foundation on which to base their caregiving, enabling them to be the best lay Christian caregivers they can be.

WHAT STEPHEN MINISTERS DO

The fundamental activity Stephen Ministers do is provide care and support for people experiencing life challenges. The care they offer is uniquely shaped by specific training and skills, as well as the well-defined boundaries that guide their ministry. This chapter will highlight the characteristics of a Stephen Minister's care, define the types of support Stephen Ministers can offer, and look at the kinds of situations they are equipped to handle.

A clear understanding of the nature of a Stephen Minister's care serves two purposes:

1) it supplies a framework for Stephen Ministers to care most effectively; and

2) it protects everyone involved from situations where Stephen Ministers would be trying to provide care beyond their abilities.

Awareness of the appropriate types of care is especially important for Stephen Ministers when it comes to mental health issues. Because such issues have the potential to affect a person's well-being and safety, Stephen Ministers need to clearly understand where the boundaries of their care lie.

Qualities of a Stephen Minister's Care

A Stephen Minister's care is defined by a number of essential qualities, as described below:

> Stephen Ministers provide high-quality, one-to-one, confidential, Christ-centered care.

These qualities are constant in every Stephen Ministry caring relationship.

High-Quality

Stephen Ministers strive to provide *high-quality* care. The excellent care that Stephen Ministers have given to hurting people since Stephen Ministry first began is one of the main reasons the ministry has been so successful, and every newly trained Stephen Minister contributes to this legacy of quality caregiving.

Several factors contribute to the high-quality care Stephen Ministers provide.

- First and foremost, it is God, the Curegiver, who empowers Stephen Ministers to care and is always present in their ministry, bringing healing through their care. The process-oriented care that all Stephen Ministers learn helps them leave room for God to work in the caring relationship—and the result is that their caregiving is far more successful than any Stephen Minister could ever manage alone.

- Stephen Ministers' thorough training is another factor that contributes to the effectiveness of their care. Because they're well prepared with knowledge, skills, and resources, Stephen Ministers can care effectively in a wide variety of situations. They also receive regular continuing education, which gives them opportunities to further improve and expand their caring skills.

- In addition, by participating in regular small group peer supervision, Stephen Ministers receive consistent support, guidance, and accountability. Stephen Ministers take seriously the responsibility to help each other maintain a high level of care for their care receivers.

- The consistency of Stephen Ministers' care is also vital in ensuring the quality of that care. By meeting with care receivers weekly, for as long as the need for care persists, Stephen Ministers provide a reliable support that care receivers can truly trust.

- Finally, the commitment Stephen Ministers make to caring as best as they can is an essential component. Without the personal dedication to implement their training and allow God to work through them, high-quality caring cannot take place.

One-to-One

Stephen Ministers provide care in the context of *one-to-one* caring relationships. The visits that make up a Stephen Minister's interactions with a care receiver do not include other people, and Stephen Ministers work to ensure the privacy of the relationship.

There are several reasons that Stephen Ministers' care happens one to one.

- The most important is that Stephen Ministers are specifically trained to care for individuals in a one-to-one setting. The skills from their training don't apply to caring for more than one person at a time—for example, couples or families.

- Another is that it allows caring visits to focus solely on the needs of the care receiver, rather than dividing the focus among multiple people. This helps the Stephen Minister delve deeper into the care receiver's situation and feelings.

- Lastly, one-to-one care makes confidentiality much easier to maintain, since everything is shared only between the care receiver and the Stephen Minister.

It's also important to note that the one-to-one care of Stephen Ministers occurs in person. The physical presence of Stephen Ministers is a key component of their caring, communicating their commitment to care receivers in a powerful way and enabling them to most effectively utilize their caregiving skills.

Confidential

As discussed in several modules of Stephen Minister training, Stephen Ministers provide *confidential* care. Here's what training module 9 has to say about the importance of confidentiality:

> Confidentiality is a cornerstone of Stephen Ministry. Without it, few people would agree to receive care, and those who did would be more reluctant to talk about what they're really thinking and feeling. . . . This assurance helps create a safe place where care receivers can openly share their most painful concerns—including those they may not discuss even with close friends or family.[1]

Module 2, "Feelings: Yours, Mine, and Ours," also describes how confidentiality serves as the roof of the Safe House that Stephen Ministers create for their care receivers.

It's an indispensable part of the caregiving process that protects the entire caring relationship and fosters a safe environment for sharing.

Simply put, without confidentiality Stephen Ministers would not be able to do what they do. The trust care receivers extend to their Stephen Ministers depends on confidentiality. As the caring relationship grows over time, that trust continues to build—allowing the care receiver and Stephen Minister to reach deeper issues.

Christ-Centered

As people motivated to ministry by their faith, Stephen Ministers are always providing *Christ-centered* care—whether or not they are engaged in specifically Christian caring activities, like prayer or reading Scripture. This reality is described in *Christian Caregiving—a Way of Life* as "a cup of cold water":

> Any time you express Jesus' love in a way that meets people's needs, you are providing Christian care. God's presence and active involvement makes every aspect of your care Christian from the start. This is true whether or not you offer distinctively Christian words along with a cup of cold water.[2]

As they offer Christ-centered care, Stephen Ministers become a channel through which God's love for the care receiver is conveyed. Whether they are caring themselves or helping a care receiver connect with help outside of Stephen Ministry, Stephen Ministers follow the example of the Good Shepherd and answer God's call to "Carry each other's burdens" (Galatians 6:2).

The Stephen Minister's Care in Practice

The way Stephen Ministers provide high-quality, one-to-one, confidential, Christ-centered care looks different in each caring relationship depending on the needs of the care receiver. That said, there are two forms of support through which Stephen Ministers' care is given—as well as two caregiving contexts in which they are best able to care.

Forms of Support Stephen Ministers Offer

For the most part, Stephen Ministers' caregiving takes two forms:

1) emotional support; and

2) spiritual support.

The caring skills Stephen Ministers learn in their training are centered on these two kinds of care, so these are the areas where they are most effective.

- Stephen Ministers provide ***emotional support*** by helping care receivers recognize, acknowledge, and talk through feelings. They use active listening, empathy, reflection, validation, and other skills to encourage care receivers to share their thoughts and emotions, offering emotional stability and consistency through their ministry of presence. Also, Stephen Ministers focus not on the results but on the process of caring, which helps care receivers work with their feelings at their own pace and in healthy ways.

- Stephen Ministers provide ***spiritual support*** by helping care receivers recognize, address, and work through various spiritual issues. They are open to discussing spiritual concerns when care receivers bring them up, and may at times gently prompt care receivers to explore the spiritual aspects of their lives. Stephen Ministers use great care when approaching spiritual topics with care receivers, following the care receiver's lead and avoiding pressuring them in this area. As appropriate, Stephen Ministers might pray, read Scripture, or use other distinctively Christian caregiving tools with their care receivers.

Two Contexts in Which Stephen Ministers Provide Care

There are two caregiving contexts in which Stephen Ministers work:

1) crisis care; and

2) long-term care.

Stephen Ministers provide comparable emotional and spiritual support in either context, although some aspects of the caring relationship differ between crisis care and long-term care situations.

- **Crisis care** is the most common type of caregiving context that Stephen Ministers are involved in. Many Stephen Ministry caring relationships begin after a precipitating event—for instance, the death of a loved one, the loss of a job, the start of divorce proceedings, or a cancer diagnosis—that has left a person in a state of crisis. The Stephen Minister then starts meeting with the person to provide care as he or she works through the crisis. That care continues for as long as the person needs it, including if additional crises arise in the person's life.

  Care in this context is typically focused on identifying a care receiver's emotional and spiritual needs and helping address those needs, including as they change over time. Stephen Ministers walk alongside care receivers throughout this process, facilitating the sharing of thoughts and reflections, empathizing with feelings, and giving encouragement and support as the care receiver works through his or her current challenges.

- **Long-term care** involves circumstances where a care receiver's situation or needs are not likely to change much over time, such as someone who is living with a chronic illness.

Care in a long-term context is usually focused on providing comfort and the ministry of presence. Because the care receiver's needs typically remain constant, rather than caring with the expectation that the situation will be fully resolved, the Stephen Minister simply focuses on meeting the ongoing needs of the person as well as possible. Depending on the length and nature of the caring relationship, both the care receiver and the Stephen Minister may benefit if a new Stephen Minister is assigned after a period of time.

Whether a caring relationship is a crisis care or long-term care situation depends on the specific circumstances of the care receiver and may change over time. For example, the caregiver of a family member with a chronic condition might initially need long-term care, but when the family member passes away, he or she is likely to need crisis care. Or, a person seriously injured in an accident might start off needing crisis care but transition to long-term care during the recovery process.

Situations Where Stephen Ministers May Provide Care

Stephen Ministers have the knowledge and skills to care for people experiencing a wide range of life difficulties. Following is a list of situations that are appropriate for Stephen Ministers.

Needs for Care Appropriate for Stephen Ministers

Grief

Divorce

Job loss

Cancer diagnosis

Medical crisis

Spiritual crisis

Stress related to being a caregiver

Hospitalization

Terminal illness

Chronic health conditions

Adjustment to disability

Separation

Miscarriage

Infertility

Pregnancy

Empty nest

Challenges related to parenting

Issues related to aging

Adjustment to retirement

Job stress

Unemployment

Relocation

Changes in living situation

Natural disaster

Military deployment of a loved one

Rehabilitation from illness or injury

Financial stress

Other life challenges

People who are closely connected to an individual experiencing any of these crises, such as family members or other loved ones, may also benefit from the care of a Stephen Minister.

Note that although these situations are ones Stephen Ministers usually can handle, it's entirely possible that a care receiver experiencing one of them may need professional help instead of or in addition to Stephen Ministry. With a few exceptions that will be discussed in the next chapter, it's not the situation itself but the care receiver's response to it that ultimately determines whether Stephen Ministry is the appropriate kind of care. Stephen Ministers care for people whose coping mechanisms are for the most part intact. If a person is unable to cope with his or her situation, that points to a need for some kind of professional care.

WHAT STEPHEN MINISTERS DO NOT DO

The training Stephen Ministers receive prepares them to be excellent caregivers for people experiencing a wide range of life crises, but that doesn't mean they can provide care in every situation. As discussed in the previous chapter, Stephen Ministers are specially trained for lay caregiving—they're equipped to give certain forms of support (emotional and spiritual) within specific contexts (crisis care and long-term care). Inside those parameters, Stephen Ministers can be highly effective.

Should Stephen Ministers go outside those forms of support or specific contexts, however, their ability to provide the best possible care for their care receivers is very likely to be compromised. This is partly a matter of practicality; if Stephen Ministers spend time and energy trying to provide other forms of support, they'll be less able to meet care receivers' emotional and spiritual needs. It's also a matter of boundaries. If Stephen Ministers attempt to offer support beyond what they're trained to do, care receivers may begin to have inaccurate expectations for the caring relationship. Plus, outside the contexts of crisis care and long-term care, Stephen Ministers can find themselves struggling to provide the high-quality care that is a defining aspect of Stephen Ministry. Most importantly, if Stephen Ministers attempt to deal with situations they're not equipped for, care receivers' well-being could be at risk.

This chapter identifies a number of specific kinds of support that Stephen Ministers do not provide and situations in which they do not serve. Many of these categories relate directly to mental health issues, which generally require professional care that Stephen Ministers are not able to provide.

Types of Support Stephen Ministers Do Not Provide

The previous chapter discussed the two forms of support that Stephen Ministers offer: emotional and spiritual. For the most part, other kinds of support lie outside the boundaries of Stephen Ministry.

There are four main forms of support that Stephen Ministers do not provide: practical, financial, social, and professional. If a care receiver requests a Stephen Minister's help or otherwise seems to need assistance in one of these areas, rather than trying to provide that support, the best response is for Stephen Ministers to help the care receiver connect with other resources that can meet those needs. Doing so guards against the boundaries of the caring relationship becoming blurred or the care receiver becoming dependent on the Stephen Minister. If Stephen Ministers are unsure about whether providing a certain kind of support is appropriate, they can talk with their Supervision Group or Stephen Leaders.

Practical Support

Practical support involves helping with day-to-day activities, such as providing transportation, doing chores or errands, assisting with childcare, or other similar tasks. Providing this type of help is outside the role of a Stephen Minister. Because many kinds of practical support are recurring (such as picking up groceries) and might be requested again in the future, a Stephen Minister's agreeing to help with these needs can require a significant amount of time and pose a particular risk to maintaining appropriate boundaries. In addition, some kinds of practical support may carry certain legal or safety risks. For all these reasons, the best way Stephen Ministers can respond to a care receiver's practical needs is to connect the person with resources outside of Stephen Ministry that can supply the assistance the care receiver needs.

Financial Support

Stephen Ministers don't exchange money with care receivers, whether by accepting payment of any kind for their ministry or by giving or lending money to their care receivers. Such transactions are wholly inappropriate for Stephen Ministry and have the potential to cause serious damage to the caring relationship.

Social Support

While Stephen Ministers may relate in friendly ways with their care receivers, the purpose of their caring relationships is to address care receivers' emotional and spiritual needs, not meet their social needs. As such, Stephen Ministers do not engage in purely social activities with care receivers, such as going to a movie together, inviting the care receiver over for dinner, or joining a gathering of the care receiver's friends. Doing so would cross the line between a Stephen Ministry caring relationship and a friendship.

Professional Support

As lay caregivers, it's important for Stephen Ministers to avoid offering any kind of support that requires professional skills or knowledge—even if the Stephen Minister possesses such professional expertise.

- Stephen Ministers do not offer support that should be provided by a professional caregiver or other qualified

What Stephen Ministers Do Not Do

individual. One clear example is in the area of mental health—Stephen Ministers do not diagnose or attempt to treat mental disorders. Sharing legal, medical, or other professional advice falls into this category as well. Whatever the specifics, providing professional support in a non-professional capacity is inappropriate for a Stephen Minister.

- Stephen Ministers also do not offer support within their own realm of professional expertise. For example, a Stephen Minister who works as an accountant wouldn't help a care receiver prepare his or her taxes, and a Stephen Minister who is a hairdresser wouldn't give haircuts to the care receiver's children. Providing these kinds of services, free or otherwise, creates boundary issues by blurring the distinction between the Stephen Minister as a lay caregiver and as a professional.

A limited exception to these guidelines is if a Stephen Minister, due to his or her professional skills or expertise, naturally recognizes a sign that a care receiver may need help in a specific area. For example, a Stephen Minister trained as a nurse might listen to a care receiver's sharing about some physical problems and, through professional experience, recognize the possible symptoms of some kind of illness. In this situation, it would be appropriate for the Stephen Minister to suggest that the care receiver see a medical professional. This exception is appropriate because the Stephen Minister does not provide a professional diagnosis or attempt to personally provide any medical care, instead suggesting that the care receiver connect with an outside resource. Similarly, a lawyer serving as a Stephen Minister could listen to a care receiver sharing about a problem with the family business, recognize a need, and suggest the care recevier get legal assistance—without the Stephen Minister giving any specific advice.

Situations in Which Stephen Ministers Do Not Serve as Caregivers

For the vast majority of potential caregiving situations, the care receiver's response to his or her circumstances and how intact his or her coping mechanisms are determines whether Stephen Ministers can appropriately offer care. However, a number of situations are by nature inappropriate for Stephen Ministry because they require specialized, professional care beyond what Stephen Ministers are equipped to offer.

Most times, Stephen Leaders' preparation interviews with potential care receivers will identify any situations inappropriate for Stephen Ministry. There are also some situations (such as those involving minors) that would be apparent even before the preparation interview happens. In such cases, a Stephen Minister wouldn't be assigned in the first place. On occasion, though, a care receiver's circumstances or needs may develop or be discovered to be beyond what a Stephen Minister can handle after a caring relationship has already started. For these reasons, it's important that Stephen Ministers be able to recognize those needs and situations that are inappropriate for Stephen Ministry.

Minors

Stephen Ministers do not provide care for minors. Because the parents or other legal guardians of a minor have a right to know what's going on with that individual, a Stephen Leader or Stephen Minister would be unable to offer confidentiality in the caring relationship. In addition, the caregiving skills Stephen Ministers learn in their training are oriented toward relating to adults and may not be as effective with younger individuals. Finally, there may be various legal concerns with an adult Stephen Minister meeting individually with a minor. For these reasons, Stephen Ministers should never be assigned to caring relationships with minors.

Couples or Families

Stephen Ministers only care for individuals in one-to-one relationships. Caring for a couple, family, or other group would make confidential sharing impossible and limit a Stephen Minister's ability to provide focused care for an individual care receiver's needs. Most importantly, the skills needed for group caregiving or helping to solve relational issues differ significantly from those of a Stephen Minister, so the quality of care would be compromised in a group setting. If multiple people in a family or group are in need of a Stephen Minister, each person should have his or her own Stephen Minister and meet with that Stephen Minister individually.

Individuals with Mental Disorders

Care receivers who have mental disorders need professional care that Stephen Ministers are not qualified to provide. The specific skills and therapeutic methods required to treat individuals experiencing these kinds of issues mean that only a mental health professional is qualified to care for someone with a mental disorder. Attempting to provide that care as a Stephen Minister would not only compromise quality of care but also potentially put people's safety at risk. Chapters 6 and 7 discuss how to recognize signs of a possible mental disorder and what steps Stephen Ministers take to connect the care receiver with the appropriate care.

Individuals Dealing with Addiction

People dealing with an addiction of any kind—whether a substance use disorder or a behavioral addiction such as gambling—need specialized care beyond what a Stephen Minister can provide and require the help of a professional.

What Stephen Ministers Do Not Do

Individuals Exhibiting Manipulative Behavior

On occasion, people who are hurting may attempt to manipulate those around them in order to meet their wants or needs. It's possible that some care receivers can be manipulative without realizing it, but others may be fully aware of what they're doing when they try to get a Stephen Minister to provide support outside the boundaries of Stephen Ministry. A single attempt at manipulation is not automatically a serious concern, although it still demands an assertive response from the Stephen Minister. When care receivers begin to demonstrate a pattern of manipulative behavior, however, there is a high risk of significant boundary issues that would interfere with the Stephen Minister's ability to provide high-quality care. Such individuals need to be referred to a professional.

Individuals Involved in Abusive Situations

Any situation involving abuse—whether a care receiver is abusing another person, is being abused, or is aware of someone being abused—is beyond what Stephen Ministers as lay caregivers can handle. These situations are extremely sensitive and require specialized care to ensure the safety and well-being of those involved. Stephen Ministers are unable to provide the needed care when someone is in an abusive situation and need to pass that information along. Many localities have mandatory reporting laws regarding abuse; these laws often apply specifically to certain categories of professionals, but in some areas everyone is considered a mandatory reporter. Stephen Ministers need to be aware of and follow the legal requirements in their area, but even if it isn't mandated by law, they have a moral obligation to involve the appropriate professionals—working in conjunction with their Stephen Ministry Crisis Contacts—if they become aware of abuse.

Individuals Exhibiting Violent Behavior

Due to safety concerns, Stephen Ministers are unable to provide care in a situation where a care receiver is threatening or exhibiting violent behavior. As lay caregivers, Stephen Ministers are not in any way equipped to deal with a person who is or may become violent. It is extremely rare for Stephen Ministers to encounter a situation like this, but if they do, they should not attempt to handle the situation themselves. Instead, they need to contact emergency services to protect their own and others' well-being.

When Stephen Ministers Cannot Provide Care, They Recognize and Refer

When a care receiver needs a type of support or is involved in a situation beyond what Stephen Ministers can handle, the role of the Stephen Minister involves two steps:

1) *recognizing* the care receiver's need for outside help; and

2) starting a process of *referring* the care receiver to a resource that can meet that need.

Sometimes it will be obvious that a care receiver needs help from another source of care; other times, it may not be so clear. Also, in some circumstances the best resource for the care receiver may not be readily apparent. Fortunately, Stephen Ministers aren't alone in navigating those uncertainties—they can turn to their Supervision Groups and Stephen Leaders for consultation about what to do.

Chapters 6 and 7 discuss these two steps—recognition and referral—with a focus on mental health issues. For more about using resources outside the area of mental health, see Stephen Minister training module 11, "Using Mental Health Professionals and Other Community Resources."

STEPHEN MINISTRY AND MENTAL HEALTH PROFESSIONALS

Stephen Ministers and mental health professionals each have a unique and valuable role in providing care for hurting people. While the type of care provided by mental health professionals differs from that of Stephen Ministers, the respective skills and goals of each can effectively complement one another. In particular, mental health professionals are a valuable resource for Stephen Ministers in situations where care receivers are experiencing mental health issues.

As chapter 1 states, the goal of Stephen Ministry is for hurting people to receive the best care possible, whether that care is provided by a Stephen Minister or someone else. In the case of mental health issues, the best possible care almost always means the care of a mental health professional, so Stephen Ministers can best achieve the goal of

Stephen Ministry by assisting care receivers in connecting with that help when such a need arises.

Ways Mental Health Professionals May Work with Stephen Ministry

There are three ways mental health professionals may work with a congregation's Stephen Ministry. Stephen Ministers can check with their Stephen Leaders for specifics about how these methods are implemented in their congregation.

1. As a Caregiver for a Care Receiver Who Needs Professional Care

The most common way mental health professionals work with Stephen Ministry is by taking on a Stephen Ministry care receiver as a client. This may occur when a Stephen Leader identifies a potential need for professional care before a Stephen Minister is assigned, or when a Stephen Minister recognizes signs that such a need may have developed after a caring relationship has begun. Exactly when and how the professional gets involved depends on the situation.

To facilitate this process, the Stephen Leader Team maintains a Community Resources Handbook that includes a number of local mental health professionals to whom referrals can be made. Before including people or organizations on the list, the Stephen Leaders will usually contact them first to make them aware of Stephen Ministry and find out if they are open to taking on Stephen Ministry care receivers as clients. This helps the process of referring a care receiver move more smoothly when the need arises.

On occasion, a care receiver may require help from a mental health professional who has not previously worked with the congregation's Stephen Ministry. In such situations, Stephen Ministers and Stephen Leaders work together with the care receiver to supply the mental health professional with key information about Stephen Ministry and facilitate a good referral.

The next three chapters of this book go into greater detail on the process of referring a care receiver to a mental health professional.

2. For Consultation about a Care Receiver's Needs

Stephen Leaders at many congregations enlist at least one mental health professional to provide consultation in situations related to the mental health of care receivers. The individuals may be congregation members or professionals from the community who have a good relationship with the congregation's Stephen Ministry. These consulting mental health professionals can help assess the mental health needs of care receivers, especially in situations where Stephen Ministers and Stephen Leaders are unsure of what to do.

3. As a Resource for Continuing Education

In some congregations, Stephen Leaders may ask mental health professionals from the congregation or community to provide continuing education to Stephen Ministers on mental health–related topics. They might teach a continuing education session themselves or take part in a panel discussion to answer Stephen Ministers' questions. Drawing on the expertise of these professionals can be an excellent opportunity for Stephen Ministers to expand their knowledge in the area of mental health. Keep in mind, though, that such teaching does not equip Stephen Ministers to make diagnoses or provide any kind of professional care.

An Introduction to the Types of Mental Health Professionals

Mental health professionals are individuals who have earned an advanced degree, typically a master's or doctorate, in a mental health field. Most of these professionals have completed practicums, internships, or other forms of supervised, hands-on training. After finishing their training, mental health professionals are typically licensed by a board representing the state or locality where they will work. Licensure, which involves passing a state licensing exam among other requirements, verifies a professional's qualifications and certifies that he or she is allowed to offer professional care. Although individual mental health professionals may have specialized skills or areas of emphasis, most practice some form of psychotherapy (also known as *talk therapy*).

Mental health professionals also typically adhere to a code of ethics set by the professional organization representing their specialty. These codes serve to guide mental health professionals in maintaining appropriate boundaries with clients.

Following are a number of types of mental health professionals, organized alphabetically.[1]

Addiction Counselors

Addiction counselors are health care professionals who treat a variety of substance and behavioral addictions. Because many addiction counselors focus on certain kinds of addictions or specific populations, titles and educational backgrounds vary across the discipline. Individual professionals use a variety of treatment methods, such as one-to-one talk therapy, group therapy, leading peer recovery groups, and diagnosing co-occurring mental health issues.

- **Education:** Varies depending on the location, specialty, and preferences of the counselor—with degrees ranging from the associate's level up through doctorates, in subjects such as addiction counseling, psychology, and social work.
- **Licensing:** Licensing for addiction counselors often depends on the type of addiction they specialize in treating. Typically, professionals who treat substance use disorders are licensed by a state addiction counseling licensing board

separate from the professional counselor licensing board. In some states, those who work with behavioral addictions such as gambling are licensed through the state's addiction counseling licensing board; in others, they are licensed as professional counselors, chemical dependency counselors, or under other titles.

- **Ethics:** NAADAC, the Association for Addiction Professionals, provides a code of ethics used by professionals in the area of addiction prevention and treatment.

Clinical Psychologists

Clinical psychologists are mental health professionals who specialize in a variety of areas related to psychology. Clinical psychologists provide "continuing and comprehensive mental and behavioral health care for individuals and families" with a wide range of needs, from relatively minor adjustment issues like midlife crises to more severe disorders like schizophrenia. The scope of clinical psychologists' work is broad, as they are equipped to care for individuals and groups of all ages, from all backgrounds, and in many different contexts.[2]

One aspect of clinical psychologists' work is their ability to use psychological testing in their diagnosis, assessment, and treatment of patients. In addition, clinical psychologists may also be involved in research related to their area of work.

- **Education:** Doctor of Philosophy (PhD) or Doctor of Psychology (PsyD).

- **Licensing:** Clinical psychologists are licensed to practice in the United States through the psychology licensure boards of their state.

- **Ethics:** The American Psychological Association (APA) provides ethical principles and a code of conduct for individuals practicing clinical psychology. These guidelines are observed by members of the APA and have been adopted by a number of other organizations as well.

Clinical Social Workers

Clinical social workers are specialists within the field of social work who focus on "the assessment, diagnosis, treatment, and prevention" of mental disorders. Their work typically involves face-to-face therapy and counseling with individuals, groups, or families, and they are able to deal with a variety of mental disorders and other related issues.[3] Depending on their work setting, they may work in conjunction with other mental health or medical professionals to provide holistic care for a client or patient.

- **Education:** Master's degree in social work (MSW), although some clinicians may obtain a doctoral degree in social work (DSW or PhD).

- **Licensing:** Clinical social workers are licensed to practice in the United States through the social work licensing board of their state. Those who complete the requirements set by these boards are known as Licensed Clinical Social Workers (LCSW).

- **Ethics:** The National Association of Social Workers provides a code of ethics used by social workers. State-specific clinical social work organizations may supplement that code with their own ethical standards. There are national organizations, such as the Clinical Social Work Association, that provide their own code of ethics specific to clinical social work; however, not all state clinical social work organizations are affiliated with these larger bodies.

Counseling Psychologists

Counseling psychologists are mental health professionals who "focus on facilitating personal and interpersonal functioning" and address the "emotional, social, vocational, education, health-related, developmental, and organizational concerns" of clients.[4] The Society of Counseling Psychology describes the difference between counseling and clinical psychologists this way: "Clinical psychologists have traditionally studied disturbances in mental health, while counseling psychologists' earliest role was to provide vocational guidance and advice. Today, though . . . there are perhaps more similarities than differences among individual psychologists from each field."[5] Despite the diminishing distinctions between the work of the two roles, these historical roots continue to shape the kinds of help each is most likely to provide.

- **Education:** Doctor of Philosophy (PhD), Doctor of Education (EdD), or Doctor of Psychology (PsyD).
- **Licensing:** Like clinical psychologists, counseling psychologists are licensed to practice in the United States through the psychology licensure boards of their state.
- **Ethics:** The American Psychological Association provides ethical principles and a code of conduct for those who practice as counseling psychologists. This is the same code of ethics provided for clinical psychologists.

Licensed Professional Counselors

Licensed professional counselors are mental health service providers who are "trained to work with individuals, families, and groups in treating mental, behavioral, and emotional problems and disorders." The term refers to a broad group of professionals who may focus on specific modes of practice such as diagnosis, treatment, and prevention of mental disorders; consultative work; and research into therapeutic methods.[6]

It's important to recognize that the terms *counselor* and *licensed professional counselor* are not always equivalent. In many states, *licensed professional counselor* is a "protected title," meaning that only individuals who have been licensed by the state in which they practice can identify themselves in that way. Some states have also made *counselor* a protected title, but in others it is a broad term that can be used by individuals offering a variety of services, whether or not they have received training in the area of mental health. The counselor licensing boards in each state can provide information regarding which titles require licensure to use and which do not.

- **Education:** Master of Arts (MA), Master of Science (MS), or an EdD or PhD in counseling.

- **Licensing:** Licensed professional counselors are licensed to practice in the United States by the professional counselor licensure board of their state.

- **Ethics:** The American Counseling Association provides a code of ethics for those in the counseling profession. The American Mental Health Counselors Association also provides a code of ethics specifically for those who are licensed clinical mental health counselors.

Marriage and Family Therapists

Marriage and family therapists are mental health professionals who are "trained in psychotherapy and family systems, and licensed to diagnose and treat mental and emotional disorders within the context of marriage, couples and family systems." These therapists specialize in providing care for people—individuals, couples, and families—with specific attention to their familial relationships. They can also address various individual mental health disorders with a focus on how the person's relationships are connected to the issue.[7]

- **Education:** MA, MS, or PhD in marriage and family therapy, although some practitioners may have a Doctor of Marriage and Family Therapy (DMFT) degree.

- **Licensing:** In most states, marriage and family therapists are licensed to practice by a marriage and family therapy licensure board. Many states' boards use the national examination conducted by the Association of Marriage and Family Therapy Regulatory Boards as a licensure requirement. Those who complete the requirements set by these boards are typically known as Licensed Marriage and Family Therapists (LMFTs), although the terminology may vary slightly from state to state.

- **Ethics:** The American Association for Marriage and Family Therapy provides a code of ethics for marriage and family therapists.

Psychiatric–Mental Health Nurses

Psychiatric–mental health nurses are specialized nurses who "work with individuals, families, groups, and communities, assessing their mental health needs . . . [developing] a nursing diagnosis and plan of care, [implementing] the nursing process, and [evaluating] it for effectiveness." Nurses working in this specialty are required to complete additional education and training beyond that of a registered nurse and typically become Advanced Practice Registered Nurses (APRNs), although titling varies by state.[8]

The role of a psychiatric–mental health nurse is a broad one informed by the unique practices and focuses of the nursing profession and typically involves a good amount of direct contact with clients. Those certified as nurse practitioners can also prescribe medication, although requirements differ depending on location. The setting of their work often informs whether these nurses specialize in treating specific mental disorders.

- **Education:** Typically a Master of Science in Nursing (MSN), although some may obtain a Doctor of Nursing Practice (DNP) degree.

- **Licensing:** Psychiatric–mental health nurses are licensed to practice in the United States by the nursing board of their state.

- **Ethics:** The American Nurses Association provides a code of ethics used by all nurses, including psychiatric–mental health nurses.

Psychiatrists

Psychiatrists are medical doctors who "[specialize] in mental health" and "are qualified to assess both the mental and physical aspects of psychological problems." Psychiatrists can prescribe medication, which they often combine with psychotherapy or other treatment methods. They also have access to medical testing that can be used as part of their diagnosis, assessment, and treatment of patients. Psychiatrists have the ability to admit patients into hospitals when needed.[9]

- **Education:** Doctor of Medicine (MD) or Doctor of Osteopathic Medicine (DO).
- **Licensing:** Psychiatrists are licensed to practice in the United States through the medical board of their state.
- **Ethics:** The American Psychiatric Association provides an ethical code used by psychiatrists.

The Two Most Important Things to Know about a Mental Health Professional

Stephen Ministers and Stephen Leaders may have a variety of questions about finding mental health professionals to whom care receivers can be referred. Ultimately, the two most important things to know about a mental health professional can be identified through two key questions:

1. Is the mental health professional competent in his or her area of care?

2. Is the mental health professional respectful of clients' religious beliefs, regardless of what they are, and willing to discuss spiritual concerns?

The most important characteristic for any mental health professional is *competence*. With the goal of Stephen Ministry in mind—ensuring that care receivers get the best care possible—it's clear that care receivers should be referred only to professionals who are able to provide excellent mental health care.

The second key characteristic is *respect for clients' religious beliefs,* which often goes hand in hand with competence. An effective mental health professional, whether Christian or non-Christian, will respect clients' religious beliefs and be willing to discuss spiritual matters if they are important to the client. It's important to have a good sense for how professionals will respond to topics of faith before deciding whether to refer care receivers to them.

Together, these two characteristics are a good indicator that a mental health professional is likely to be a good fit for the needs of Stephen Ministry care receivers. So, identifying whether a professional might be a good fit for working with Stephen Ministry care receivers can be relatively simple: If a mental health professional is both competent and respectful of clients' religious beliefs, Stephen Leaders and Stephen Ministers can feel confident in referring a care receiver to him or her.

WHEN TO REFER A CARE RECEIVER TO A MENTAL HEALTH PROFESSIONAL

When care receivers need care beyond the scope of Stephen Ministry, the role of the Stephen Minister is to *recognize* that need and then work with others to *refer* the care receiver to an outside resource that can meet that need. This chapter deals with the first of these steps: recognizing when care receivers might need the care of a mental health professional.

The next chapter will describe the process Stephen Ministers use to work with their Stephen Leaders to refer care receivers to professional care.

Recognizing When a Referral May Be Needed

This section describes a number of signs and situations that indicate a care receiver may need to be referred to a mental health professional. While these signs are often associated with mental health issues, it's also possible that they may point to a need for a different kind of care. This is why Stephen Ministers work together with their Supervision Group or Stephen Leaders to consider the specifics of each situation.

When Stephen Ministers see signs like those listed in this section, they can confidently and assertively initiate the process of working with their Supervision Group or Stephen Leaders to decide on the best course of action. Stephen Ministers do not have to—and should not—take sole responsibility for determining the exact kind of professional help a care receiver needs. Instead, they can simply be alert to any signs and share their concerns in order to ensure care receivers get the appropriate type and level of care.

Signs That a Care Receiver May Need to Be Referred

Following are a number of signs that indicate that a care receiver may need the help of a mental health professional.

- **Decreased Ability to Function in Daily Life:** This sign involves lacking the interest or capacity to complete necessary daily activities, such as essential household chores, basic personal hygiene, eating, or sleeping; not keeping up with important responsibilities, such as going to work or school; or being unable to maintain relationships or communicate with others. It may also entail a person withdrawing from enjoyable activities or isolating him- or herself. Of particular concern are situations where an individual who was previously functioning adequately begins to experience significant difficulties in these areas.

- **Inability to Adapt to Crisis:** Most people have a number of familiar coping strategies they rely on to maintain a state of mental and emotional stability in the midst of difficult situations. For example, a person might take walks, spend time journaling, or talk with a trusted friend or family member when feeling stressed or anxious. As discussed in module 8 of Stephen Minister training, "Crisis Theory and Practice," people who have experienced a precipitating event leading to a state of crisis find that their customary ways of dealing with change are not sufficient for reducing their current stress and anxiety, requiring them to find new ways of responding to regain their sense of equilibrium. This process may take time, but it is a normal response to a stressful or traumatic event and does not by itself indicate a need for professional help. However, if a person in a state of crisis seems completely unable to process the changes, adapt, and move toward growth and greater wholeness, it's a cause for concern—and possibly for referral.

- **Reckless or Self-Destructive Behavior:** Sometimes, a person in crisis will avoid or deny the need to change and adapt to their new circumstances in life, turning instead to reckless or self-destructive behavior in an attempt to relieve pain, stress, and anxiety. Such potentially harmful actions might include compulsive gambling or shopping, sabotaging important relationships, pursuing unhealthy relationships, binge eating, or extreme procrastination. Other behaviors indicate a stronger need to refer, such as signs of alcohol or substance use. These kinds of self-destructive behaviors may consist of a single dangerous decision, or they might involve a pattern of reckless activity. Whatever the specifics, a care receiver who begins to behave in ways that threaten his or her well-being needs help beyond what a Stephen Minister can offer.

- **Extreme Emotional Difficulties:** When a person's emotional difficulties manifest in extreme ways, they may point to a need for the care of a mental health professional. These kinds of difficulties might take the form of intense emotional displays, such as sudden, severe mood swings, an uncharacteristically short temper, overwhelming anxiety, or panic attacks. They can also involve an extreme lack of emotional response, including numbness, apathy, or even feeling completely emotionless.

- **Distorted Perception of Reality:** This sign occurs when what a person says or does indicates that he or she is not fully in touch with reality. One example is what pioneering psychiatrist Aaron T. Beck and his student David Burns called *cognitive distortions,* irrational beliefs or faulty ways of thinking that negatively impact a person's mental health. These include jumping to conclusions, exaggerating the negative aspects of a situation, using self-deprecating labels for oneself, blaming oneself without justification, and others.[1] While it's normal for people to have thoughts like these on occasion, they become problematic when they begin to dominate a person's thinking and become so pervasive that they prevent the individual from responding to situations in a rational way.

  More extreme examples of a distorted perception of reality include auditory or visual hallucinations, an inability to distinguish between past and present, or paranoia.

- **Overdependence:** One way a care receiver may try to compensate for ineffective coping mechanisms is by looking to or relying on the Stephen Minister for types of support that Stephen Ministers are unable to provide. This overdependence is often accompanied by an inability to function in daily life, with the care receiver requesting the Stephen Minister's help for activities that could reasonably be handled alone. Often it's enough for the Stephen Minister to guard against this behavior by assertively maintaining boundaries, but when a care receiver consistently attempts to push the boundaries of the caring relationship despite the Stephen Minister's efforts or becomes manipulative, he or she may be moving toward overdependence and need professional help.

- **A Downward Spiral:** A downward spiral occurs when a person becomes progressively less able to cope with his or her circumstances. A spiral may result when a person is no longer able to handle an existing crisis or when additional crises occur on top of a current crisis. This struggle may be intensified by pervasive negative thinking, possibly including self-blame, despair, and depression. Typically, many of the other signs previously discussed are also present. Overall, a person in a downward spiral may seem out of control of life and increasingly unable to mentally, emotionally, and spiritually deal with what he or she is experiencing.

- **Physical Problems:** There are a number of physical signs that may be related to a mental disorder, such as rapid weight loss or gain, frequent headaches or migraines, inability to sleep, and fatigue. It's possible, though, that such symptoms may be the result of an illness or physical disorder, so it's helpful to assess whether other signs of possible mental health issues are present along with any physical issues when considering what kind of care might be most appropriate.

One overall sign to watch for is changes in patterns of behavior, which can appear in conjunction with any of the signs above. For example, a care receiver who has been self-sufficient might abruptly start to push the boundaries of the caring relationship and move toward overdependence. Or, a care receiver who was moderately depressed could share that he or she has started drinking to help numb his or her painful feelings. These kinds of sudden shifts may indicate that the care receiver's ability to maintain his or her current level of mental health has deteriorated.

Although these signs can be indicators of a mental disorder, it's critical that Stephen Ministers do *not* use them to attempt to make a clinical diagnosis. Rather, Stephen Ministers should consider observations of any of these signs an indication that they need to consult with others. With the support and help of their Supervision Group or Stephen Leaders, Stephen Ministers can think through the care receiver's potential need for professional help—ensuring that care receivers are connected with the kind of care most appropriate for their needs.

Specific Situations in Which Stephen Ministers Always Refer

While the signs in the previous section indicate a possible need for a mental health professional's care, there are a few types of situations that *always* require a referral to professional help.

- **Severe Depression:** While Stephen Ministry is appropriate for individuals who are experiencing mild or moderate depression, Stephen Ministers are not able to provide care for people who have severe depression. These care receivers need to be referred to a mental health professional. Stephen Minister training module 13, "Caring for Those with Depression: The Stephen Minister's Role," covers the signs of depression and how to recognize when a care receiver's depression may have progressed to the point of becoming severe.

- **Addictions:** If a care receiver is dealing with an addiction of any sort, he or she needs to receive care from a resource outside Stephen Ministry. Stephen Ministers are not equipped to provide the care needed to help someone overcome an addiction, so their responsibility is to consult with their Stephen Leaders to connect the care receiver with the right kind of help.

- **Safety Risks:** If a care receiver's or another person's safety is at risk, Stephen Ministers must involve professionals.

Situations involving self-harm, suicidal ideation (covered in Stephen Minister training module 14, "Understanding Suicide: How to Help People Get the Care They Need"), threats of violence from or toward a care receiver, or abuse are all outside the scope of Stephen Ministry. Depending on how immediate the risk is, Stephen Ministers may need to involve emergency services first, with other professionals getting involved later on.[2]

Navigating the Gray Area of Mental Health Referrals

When it comes to mental health issues, Stephen Ministers sometimes find themselves in a gray area. While some situations—such as when a care receiver is having suicidal thoughts—clearly call for a specific response, others will be more ambiguous. On occasion, Stephen Ministers may recognize one or more signs that a care receiver may need professional care but not know how serious the situation is. This ambiguity can leave Stephen Ministers wondering how certain they need to be before starting the process of referring a care receiver to a mental health professional.

The short answer is that Stephen Ministers can and should begin the process anytime they see signs that a care receiver *may* need professional care; they don't need to have total certainty before taking action. As the graphic on the following page shows, whenever Stephen Ministers find themselves in a gray area and aren't sure whether or not a care receiver needs the care of a mental health professional, they go ahead and seek consultation to explore the possibility of referring. In other words, if Stephen Ministers find themselves having thoughts like, "My care receiver might need professional care, but I'm not sure," or "Maybe my care receiver could use professional help, but I might be overthinking it," they take that as a sign to start the process, beginning by consulting with their Supervision Group and Stephen Leaders.

When to Refer a Care Receiver to a Mental Health Professional

The Importance of Responding Assertively to Possible Needs for Professional Care

At times, Stephen Ministers may be uncomfortable taking action based on their observations that a care receiver may need professional care. Even though they don't diagnose care receivers as having mental disorders, they might worry that they are overreacting, making assumptions, or unfairly doubting their care receiver's ability to work through any issues.

It's essential, however, that Stephen Ministers do not allow these kinds of concerns to prevent them from discussing a possible need for professional help with their Supervision Group or Stephen Leaders. The goal of Stephen Ministry is for care receivers to get the best possible care, so Stephen Ministers need to courageously and assertively take action when there's a possible caring need that falls outside Stephen Ministry.

Here are a few thoughts Stephen Ministers can keep in mind as encouragement to respond assertively to a potential need for professional care:

- The first step of the process of referring is always consultation—with the Supervision Group or Stephen Leaders—so Stephen Ministers won't end up making the final decision on their own.

- Stephen Ministers are not responsible for diagnosing the care receiver, so absolute certainty isn't needed to start the process. Rather, the Stephen Minister's role is to simply recognize the possibility of mental health issues and then involve those who can help decide what kind of help is most appropriate for the care receiver's needs.

- Exploring the possibility of a referral has no immediate effect on the caring relationship. Stephen Ministers continue to provide high-quality care during caring visits while working the process of consulting with others.

- Even when Stephen Ministers consult with others in their Supervision Groups, they still follow the same principles of confidentiality they would at any other time in the caring relationship (i.e., never using the care receiver's name).

- When a care receiver may need help and support from a professional, the most caring thing a Stephen Minister can do is to recognize that need and help the care receiver connect with that care. A successful referral to a mental health professional is a sign of great care on the part of the Stephen Minister.

Ultimately, Stephen Ministers are responsible for overcoming any hesitations they may have about starting the process of possibly referring a care receiver to a mental health professional. Whether they address their reservations by talking more with the care receiver to gather additional information about his or her needs or consulting with their Supervision Group, they must do what's necessary to overcome anything that may prevent them from responding to their observations. The only option they cannot choose is to do nothing.

Referrals to Resources Other than Mental Health Professionals

Depending on what the care receiver is experiencing, a resource other than a mental health professional may sometimes be most appropriate. For example, many physical symptoms and some cognitive issues may be the result of a physical condition rather than a mental disorder. In situations like these, a physician could best provide the help a care receiver needs. Likewise, needs for forms of support that Stephen Ministers do not offer—practical, financial, social, or professional—may require the involvement of other caregivers or organizations.

Whatever the specifics, though, the basic process of recognizing needs and referring care receivers to the appropriate resource remains the same: Whenever Stephen Ministers recognize that a care receiver needs help from a resource outside of Stephen Ministry, they look first to their Supervision Group and Stephen Leaders for consultation.

An Important Principle about Referrals

Finally, remember that referring a care receiver to a mental health professional does not mean that a Stephen Minister has failed. Rather, recognizing and responding to the care receiver's needs fulfills the purpose of Stephen Ministry. Here's what one Stephen Minister had to say about referring her care receiver to a mental health professional:

> "It was hard for me to approach my Stephen Leader and bring up my care receiver's possible need for professional help. Even knowing that God is the Curegiver, I couldn't help but think that I was failing my care receiver or wasn't doing what I needed to be doing. But after the referral, I started seeing the changes in my care receiver, and it just clicked that God knew what he was doing the whole time."

As one psychologist and Stephen Leader said, "Part of being the best caregiver they can be is for Stephen Ministers to recognize when a person might need mental health care. They're there to walk with people, but what's beyond their ability should be passed on to professionals. That's the caring thing to do."

When a care receiver is dealing with a mental health issue, the most caring, Christian response is to refer the person to a professional so he or she can get the appropriate care. Doing so demonstrates a firm understanding of a Stephen Minister's role and ultimately promotes the well-being of all involved.

HOW TO REFER A CARE RECEIVER TO A MENTAL HEALTH PROFESSIONAL

As described in chapter 6, when a care receiver may have a need for professional care, the role of the Stephen Minister is to *recognize* that possible need and initiate the process of *referring* the care receiver to a mental health professional who can meet that need. This chapter describes how Stephen Ministers work together with their Supervision Groups and Stephen Leaders to refer care receivers to mental health professionals.

Five Steps for Referring a Care Receiver to a Mental Health Professional

Upon recognizing one or more signs that a care receiver may need the help of a mental health professional, Stephen

WHEN AND HOW TO USE MENTAL HEALTH RESOURCES

Ministers initiate a five-step process to see that the care receiver gets the appropriate kind of care.

> **A Five-Step Process for Referring a Care Receiver to a Mental Health Professional**
>
> **1**
> Get Consultation
>
> **2**
> Create a List of Referral Options
>
> **3**
> Talk with the Care Receiver
>
> **4**
> Help the Care Receiver Contact the Mental Health Professional
>
> **5**
> Follow Up as Necessary

Step 1: Get Consultation

The first thing Stephen Ministers do after identifying that a care receiver may need the help of a mental health professional is consult with others to decide on the best course of action. Depending on the urgency of the situation and the Stephen Minister's level of certainty about the care receiver's need for professional help, the Stephen Minister may consult with one or more of three groups.

How to Refer a Care Receiver to a Mental Health Professional

- **Community Resource Contacts:** The first choice for consultation should be the Stephen Ministry's Community Resource Contacts. These individuals are Stephen Leaders, often including the Referrals Coordinator, whose role is to help Stephen Ministers connect their care receivers with community resources, including mental health resources. Community Resource Contacts can help with any situation involving the mental health of care receivers—whether a Stephen Minister is unsure about a care receiver's needs, certain that a care receiver needs professional help, or somewhere in between. They can also bring in a congregation's consulting mental health professional to help determine what kind of care might be most appropriate for a care receiver.[1]

- **Supervision Group:** As with other kinds of challenges that might arise in a caring relationship, the Supervision Group can be a useful resource when a Stephen Minister notices signs that a care receiver may need to be referred to a mental health professional. Supervision Groups are good for consultation in non-urgent situations when it's unclear whether a care receiver needs professional care or not. The group can help the Stephen Minister think through interactions with and observations about the care receiver, as well as provide ideas for additional questions to ask the care receiver or signs to look for.

- **Crisis Contacts:** In an emergency where the safety of the care receiver or another person is at risk, a Stephen Minister should call emergency services and then get in touch with the Stephen Ministry's Crisis Contacts. Crisis Contacts are Stephen Leaders or other church staff, often the Referrals Coordinator and a pastor, who are able to provide support to Stephen Ministers in serious situations that require an urgent response.[2]

Consultation is an indispensable part of the process of making a mental health referral. As one Stephen Leader said, "Sometimes Stephen Ministers can be nervous about situations involving a care receiver's mental health, so it's important for them to know that they won't be dealing with these situations alone. Using their Supervision Group or Stephen Leaders to discuss the situation can be comforting and helps ensure the care receiver is connected with the care they need."

Getting consultation provides Stephen Ministers the opportunity to gain additional perspectives and insights beyond their own observations and impressions. Although Stephen Ministers are able to identify possible signs of a need for professional help, it is beyond the scope of their training and ministry to make a decision about a referral to a mental health professional on their own. Consulting with others—whether the Community Resource Contacts, Supervision Groups, Crisis Contacts, or some combination of them—is essential to make sure care receivers are connected with the right kind of help.

Regardless of with whom they initially consult, Stephen Ministers will eventually work with their Community Resource Contacts to come to a final decision about whether a referral to a mental health professional or some other resource will best meet the care receiver's needs. The Community Resource Contacts will then continue to support the Stephen Minister throughout the rest of the process.

Step 2: Create a List of Referral Options

After determining that a care receiver needs the care of a mental health professional, the Stephen Minister works with the Community Resource Contacts to create a short list of possible mental health professionals to share with the care receiver. To do this, the Community Resource Contacts and Stephen Minister will typically use the Community Resource Handbook maintained by the congregation's Stephen Ministry. This resource contains information about community mental health professionals who have been carefully assessed by the Stephen Leader Team and identified as good options for referrals.

Here are a couple of guidelines for creating a list of referral options:

- **Keep the care receiver's needs in mind.** The mental health professionals selected for the list should be able to effectively meet the care receiver's specific needs. Many mental health professionals specialize in particular areas, so considering the care receiver's unique situation can help identify those professionals who may be especially well suited to the situation.

- **Limit the options to no more than two or three professionals.** The goal of the list is to provide the care receiver with a few different choices without being overwhelming. Most of the time, suggesting two or three possibilities is ideal.

Along with the names and credentials of the mental health professionals, the list can also include other relevant material, such as contact information, fees, insurance accepted, available hours, location, areas of specialization, and possibly therapeutic approaches and methods. Try also to think through what questions the care receiver is likely to have. The easier it is for the care receiver to consider the options and come to a decision, the more willing to connect with a mental health professional he or she is likely to be.

Step 3: Talk with the Care Receiver

Once a list of mental health professional options has been created, the Stephen Minister, Community Resource Contacts, and occasionally another Stephen Leader or the pastor will determine together who should talk with the care receiver about receiving professional help. Many times, the Stephen Minister is the best choice because of the existing relationship with the care receiver. Having the Stephen Minister make the suggestion can put the care receiver at ease and help him or her be receptive to the idea of receiving professional help.

Remain open to the possibility, though, that a Stephen Leader or the pastor might be the ideal person to handle the conversation. If one of these individuals has a strong relationship with the care receiver and is already aware of the situation, or if the care receiver is more likely to follow the recommendation of someone perceived as an authority figure, that person may be able to most effectively encourage the care receiver to get professional care.

This conversation is an important one, so it's vital that the discussion be positive and productive. The following process can help ensure that the conversation is as successful as possible.

1. **Pray for God's guidance and help.** Take time to pray before talking with the care receiver. Ask God to give you the words to say, a heart to listen and empathize, and the courage to be assertive in your recommendation of professional care. God always walks alongside you in your caring ministry, and seeking God's help before the conversation can help provide encouragement and diminish any anxiety you might have.

2. **Think about what to say ahead of time.** It's often helpful to spend some time beforehand to think about how you'll talk with your care receiver about a referral to a mental health professional. That might include independent reflection and possibly a practice conversation with your Community Resource Contacts. Of course, you'll want to sound natural and genuine rather than formal and rehearsed, but some advance preparation can help you feel more confident about communicating what you need to.

   In particular, avoid wording that could make the referral to a mental health professional sound drastic or alarming, such as emotionally charged language, statements that sound judgmental, jargon that could confuse the care receiver, or anything that implies a diagnosis of a specific mental disorder. Staying away from this kind of language will help your recommendation of professional help sound reasonable and non-threatening.

3. **Express care and concern for the care receiver.** When it comes time to have the conversation with the care receiver, begin by expressing care and concern. Reflect on some of the challenges and struggles the care receiver has been experiencing. Communicate your desire for the care receiver to get the best possible care. As the conversation proceeds, do your best to remain calm and non-anxious and continue to relate in a warm, caring, straightforward, and genuine manner. The more you're able to relax and

treat the referral as something normal, rather than making it seem like a big deal, the more likely it is that your care receiver will be able to relax as well.

4. **Make the recommendation.** A simple statement like, "I think you would benefit from talking with a mental health professional," is often the best way to make the initial recommendation. Being clear and assertive with this statement is important, as it avoids any potential misunderstanding about what you're recommending.

   Next, share the reason why you believe professional care would benefit the care receiver. One good way to do this is by using the care receiver's own words. For example, you might say something like, "You told me at our last meeting that you feel out of control and that you can't cope with stress like you used to." Reflecting what the care receiver has previously shared helps the care receiver feel understood and see why a mental health professional's care would be beneficial.

   It's also good to remind the care receiver of the limits of your role as a Stephen Minister. You might say something like, "As a Stephen Minister, I've gone through a lot of training, but there are limits to the types of care I can provide. I want you to get the best care you possibly can, and I think a mental health professional would be best able to meet your needs at this time." A statement like this can help prevent potential defensiveness, as it shifts some of the focus off the care receiver and puts it on the boundaries of your caregiving.

5. **Listen to the care receiver's response.** At this point, listen well to the care receiver's response. Some care receivers will be open to or even relieved by the suggestion of connecting with a mental health professional, while others may have hesitations or become defensive. Whatever the care receiver's reaction, use your Stephen Minister skills to actively listen, reflect, validate, and ask open-ended and follow-up questions. Help the care receiver explore his or her response to the idea of receiving professional care while remaining positive and assertive about the benefits it can have for the care receiver.

Care receivers may have a variety of questions about professional care. They may need affirmation that it will really help, wonder whether a mental health professional will respect their beliefs, or want to know how the referral may affect the Stephen Ministry caring relationship. Respond to the care receiver's questions kindly, confidently, and honestly. If you're unsure about something, it's okay to say, "I don't know the answer to that, but I'll find out and let you know." The key is to communicate in a caring, open way that addresses the care receiver's concerns and helps alleviate any anxiety about the idea of getting professional help.

6. **Assertively help the care receiver commit to connecting with a mental health professional.** Your ultimate goal for this conversation is for the care receiver to choose to contact a mental health professional and take ownership of that decision. As you listen, reflect, and answer questions, pay attention to what the care receiver seems to be thinking and feeling. Address any concerns and speak positively about the referral so the care receiver will feel comfortable and willing to take action. Once you've done a lot of good listening, you can share the list of mental health professionals you created and let the care receiver know that you've included a few different options to choose from.

   Because Stephen Ministers are trained to focus on the process of caring—and having the care receiver accept professional help is a results goal—they can sometimes feel uncomfortable with this step. This is an understandable discomfort, but a mental health referral is a rare instance when the best way to ensure high-quality care is to focus on a concrete result. Keep in mind that you are making the recommendation to connect with a mental health professional based on consultation with others and because professional care is what can best meet the care receiver's needs. You can rest assured that you are acting in the care receiver's best interests, out of concern for his or her well-being.

It's critical that the care receiver take ownership of this decision. A care receiver who has willingly chosen to connect with a mental health professional, rather than doing so reluctantly or to please the Stephen Minister, is far more likely to follow through on making the contact, engage in the process of receiving professional care, and benefit from that care.

Remember that it is ultimately the care receiver's choice whether to get professional help or not. You cannot force a care receiver to connect with a mental health professional. Certainly be assertive in your recommendation and confident in expressing your belief that the care receiver will benefit from the care of a professional, but recognize that it's up to the care receiver to choose to accept professional help.

Every conversation about a referral to a mental health professional is different, but using this process as a guide goes a long way toward ensuring the conversation goes well and achieves the goal of getting the care receiver connected with professional help. For additional ideas and examples of how to talk with a care receiver when referring to a mental health professional, see appendix A, "What to Say—and What Not to Say—When Referring a Care Receiver to a Mental Health Professional."

Step 4: Help the Care Receiver Contact the Mental Health Professional

It's best for the care receiver to be the one to contact the mental health professional. There are several reasons for this. First, it helps the care receiver take ownership of the decision to receive professional care, which makes it more likely that the person will follow through on his or her commitment to receive care. Second, it sets the expectation that the care receiver is responsible for getting the needed care. Finally, some mental health professionals will not accept a referral if the patient does not contact the professional him- or herself. One clinical social worker shared, "Often, mental health professionals want the person in need to be the one to call their office, because it means the person is committed to improving their mental health and taking action to do so."

The Stephen Minister's continued care can be very important during this step. Even if the care receiver has committed to contacting a mental health professional and has taken ownership of the decision, he or she may still be nervous about making the first call or going to the first appointment. The Stephen Minister can use all the caregiving tools at his or her disposal to support the care receiver—listening to feelings and concerns, validating, affirming, and providing encouragement throughout.

Sometimes, a care receiver may ask a Stephen Minister to be there when the care receiver calls the mental health

WHEN AND HOW TO USE MENTAL HEALTH RESOURCES

professional's office. The Stephen Minister can feel free to agree to that request but should be clear that he or she will only be there to provide support, not to conduct the call for the care receiver.

Step 5: Follow Up

While some care receivers may be open to contacting a mental health professional right away, others will need time to think about it and handle practical matters such as checking their schedule. In this situation, the Stephen Minister should let the care receiver know that he or she will follow up.

Assertiveness is key when following up, as the care receiver may have second thoughts about receiving professional help. If this happens, it may be necessary for the Stephen Minister to gently but firmly remind the care receiver of his or her commitment to get professional help, along with the benefits of doing so.

When to follow up after the initial conversation depends on the specific situation and relationship between the Stephen Minister and the care receiver. The Stephen Minister needs to be persistent in following up without coming across as overbearing or pressuring the care receiver. A good rule of thumb is to wait a few of days after the initial conversation and then to follow up by phone. Should the care receiver have changed his or her mind about connecting with a professional in the meantime, it's best not to discuss that right away over the phone. Instead, wait until the next caring visit to have that conversation in person.

If, after the initial commitment, a care receiver goes more than a week without at least making an initial contact with a mental health professional, the Stephen Minister should reach out to a Stephen Leader or pastor for help with encouraging the care receiver to follow through.

Responding to a Care Receiver's Reluctance to Get Help from a Mental Health Professional

Sometimes a care receiver will be reluctant or refuse to contact a mental health professional during the initial referral conversation. In these situations, two important principles seem to be competing: 1) the need to help the care receiver get the appropriate kind of care and 2) the importance of allowing the care receiver to decide for him- or herself to get professional care rather than being forced into doing so.

The Stephen Minister should keep in mind that, in the end, the decision to contact a mental health professional belongs to the care receiver. If the care receiver ultimately declines to receive care from a mental health professional, the Stephen Minister cannot force him or her to do so—and it wouldn't be helpful to try to do so anyway. But in many situations where the care receiver is initially reluctant to get help, the Stephen Minister may be able to help the care receiver think about the recommendation, become more open to the idea of getting professional help, and possibly reconsider his or her decision.

Here are some strategies a Stephen Minister can use if a care receiver is reluctant to connect with a mental health professional:

- **Find out the care receiver's reasons.** If a care receiver does not want to be referred to a mental health professional, always start by inviting and listening to the care receiver's thoughts and feelings. It may be that the person is afraid, is struggling to accept his or her need for professional help, has had a bad experience in the past, is worried about the stigma of getting help, or has other concerns that he or she needs to talk through. Take time to listen to the care receiver's thoughts so you can determine how best to address those concerns.

- **Let the care receiver know you are not equipped to provide the care he or she needs.** An assertive approach to a care receiver's reluctance includes honestly letting the care receiver know that you simply don't have the training required to meet his or her needs. You might say something like, "My goal is for you to get the best care you can, and I'm just not trained for the kind of care you need. But a professional who has more training would be able to do that." Statements like these communicate your care for the care receiver while also clearly stating that you are not able to meet his or her needs and encouraging him or her to seek professional help.

- **Normalize the care receiver's need.** Sometimes, care receivers are resistant to the idea of professional help because it conflicts with their self-concept as a whole and healthy person. They may think that seeing a mental health professional means admitting that they are "crazy" or "unstable." If you sense that your care receiver has this kind of hesitation, it can help to normalize his or her need by saying something like, "We all go through difficult times in life, and there are times when we all need help. Needing help just means we're human." Words like these can help the care receiver see their need for professional help as just an area in which they need assistance for a while, rather than as a personal flaw.

- **Compare the referral to something the care receiver is familiar with.** If the care receiver has misgivings due to fear of the unknown or a perceived stigma toward seeking help for mental health, it can be helpful to make a comparison to something the care receiver is familiar with. For example, you could say, "If you had pneumonia or a broken arm, you would certainly go to a doctor to help you recover. Seeing a mental health professional is the same—it's going to a professional who has the expertise

WHEN AND HOW TO USE MENTAL HEALTH RESOURCES

and resources to help you heal." Comparisons like this can help reduce the care receiver's anxiety.

- **When necessary, be very direct.** If you've listened and used these strategies but the care receiver still refuses to get professional care, it may be necessary to just be straightforward and direct. If nothing else has worked, you may need to say something like the following: *"[Name],* I care for you a great deal and want you to get the best care possible. I believe a mental health professional is the only one who can adequately meet your needs right now, so I'd like for you to agree to contact one of the professionals I've suggested." When you make a firm statement like this, you communicate both how deeply you care for your care receiver and how seriously you take the situation. This may get through to a care receiver when nothing else seems to, helping him or her realize that you are only recommending the referral because you truly believe it's for his or her well-being.

It doesn't happen frequently, but sometimes, despite a Stephen Minister's best efforts, a care receiver may still be unwilling to meet with a mental health professional. If this happens, the Stephen Minister should communicate that he or she will need to follow up with the congregation's Stephen Leaders. Then, after the conversation has ended, the Stephen Minister should meet with the Community Resource Contacts to discuss what to do next.

Depending on the situation, the best way to respond to a care receiver's refusal can vary. Sometimes, a Stephen Leader or pastor will meet with the care receiver to encourage him or her to get professional help. Or, they may bring in the congregation's consulting mental health professional to discuss what course of action to take. If a care receiver still refuses to get help after all these steps, the Stephen Ministry caring relationship will need to be brought to a close since the care receiver's needs are beyond what the Stephen Minister is able to handle.

When a Care Receiver Ends Up Not Needing the Care of a Mental Health Professional

It may be that during the first step of the process of referring a care receiver, getting consultation, the Stephen Minister and others may determine that the care receiver does not need to receive care from a mental health professional. Instead, the Stephen Minister might recommend some other kind of resource to the care receiver, or the caring relationship may continue as usual, with the Stephen Minister continuing to observe the care receiver for signs of a need for professional help. In a situation like this, the Supervision Group becomes especially important in helping the Stephen Minister process observations and reassess the care receiver's needs as time goes on.

AFTER A REFERRAL TO A MENTAL HEALTH PROFESSIONAL HAS BEEN MADE

Once a care receiver has begun meeting with a mental health professional, the Stephen Minister can—and should—feel good about having helped the care receiver get much-needed care. One licensed professional counselor and Stephen Leader put it this way:

"The care of a Stephen Minister can do so much good for care receivers. But at the same time, it's not the same as the care of a mental health professional. So when a Stephen Minister sees that a care receiver needs that greater level of assistance and helps the care receiver connect with it, the Stephen Minister is doing truly amazing work."

Working the process of referring to a mental health professional is a deeply caring way to ensure a care receiver gets the best possible care.

At the same time, the caring relationship doesn't automatically end after the care receiver begins meeting with a mental health care provider. Following the completion of a referral, there are a few different directions a Stephen Ministry caring relationship may take. It's important for Stephen Ministers to be aware of these possibilities and communicate them to the care receiver to set appropriate expectations and facilitate a positive transition to the care of the mental health professional.

Directions a Caring Relationship May Take after a Referral to a Mental Health Professional

Once a care receiver has established a relationship with a mental health professional, that professional—not the Stephen Minister—is the care receiver's primary caregiver. This means that the professional's expert opinion takes precedence and that the Stephen Minister should abide by his or her recommendations and decisions. It also means that it is up to the mental health professional to decide whether or not it's appropriate for the Stephen Ministry caring relationship to continue. This is part of why it's so important that mental health professionals have a clear

After a Referral to a Mental Health Professional Has Been Made

understanding of what Stephen Ministry is and know when a client has a Stephen Minister: so they can make an informed decision about what will result in the best overall care for the care receiver.

There are three possible directions a Stephen Ministry caring relationship may go following a referral to a mental health professional:

1) The caring relationship continues alongside the mental health professional's care.

2) The caring relationship pauses for a while, to be resumed at an appropriate time.

3) The Stephen Ministry caring relationship closes.

Regardless of which direction a caring relationship takes, this time of transition can be challenging for both care receivers and Stephen Ministers. As always, the Stephen Minister should focus on the process of caring by listening, reflecting, and validating any feelings the care receiver may be having about the referral. It's also important that the Stephen Minister continue to communicate positively about the referral and the care receiver's mental health professional, which can help the care receiver be fully receptive to the professional's care. If the Stephen Minister has difficult thoughts or feelings about the referral, he or she should talk about those emotions with his or her Supervision Group—not the care receiver.

WHEN AND HOW TO USE MENTAL HEALTH RESOURCES

1. The Caring Relationship Continues

Sometimes, a mental health professional will recommend that the care receiver continue to meet with his or her Stephen Minister while receiving professional care, believing it will be beneficial for the care receiver. Here's what a licensed clinical social worker had to say:

> "When I start meeting with clients, we always look at the strengths and weaknesses of their support system together. A Stephen Minister is often on the strengths side, because that's another part of their support system. When someone is going through a difficult time, it's a wonderful thing to know that a Stephen Minister is there to talk and be with them."

A licensed counselor also shared this thought: "A Stephen Ministry caring relationship provides a structured, intentional time that focuses on the care receiver outside of the therapy session. This gives the care receiver another person to talk with and can reduce feelings of isolation." Because of the additional emotional and spiritual support Stephen Ministers offer, a mental health professional may recommend that Stephen Ministry continue alongside his or her own care.

See "Providing Care Concurrently with a Mental Health Professional" on pages 109–111 for considerations to keep in mind when caring for a care receiver who is also seeing a mental health professional.

2. The Caring Relationship Pauses for a Time

Another possibility is that the mental health professional will recommend that the caring relationship pause for a while and then resume later on. This typically occurs when a care receiver is experiencing a serious mental health crisis but may recover relatively soon. The mental health professional may want to be the care receiver's exclusive caregiver during the immediate crisis or while addressing specific issues and then, once the care receiver has stabilized, involve the Stephen Minister again to help support the care receiver's continued recovery.

This is one scenario where the mental health professional may decide it's beneficial to get permission from the care receiver to communicate directly with the Stephen Minister or Stephen Leaders to discuss relevant information. Depending on the specific situation and expected duration of the pause, the Stephen Minister and Stephen Leaders may also consider whether it would be better to wait to resume the caring relationship or close the current caring relationship for the time being. As soon as these decisions have been made, they should be communicated to the care receiver as well.

3. The Caring Relationship Closes

Depending on the care receiver's diagnosis and the mental health professional's preferences and assessment of the care receiver's needs, the professional may determine that it's best for the care receiver that the Stephen Ministry caring relationship close. This may happen right after the referral is made or later on, after the mental health professional and Stephen Minister have provided care concurrently for a while.

Closure in this context can be difficult for both the care receiver and the Stephen Minister, particularly when they have had a lengthy caring relationship. However, because the decision to close the caring relationship is based on what will result in the best care for the care receiver, it's vital that the Stephen Minister support and affirm the mental health professional's decision, particularly when talking with the care receiver.

When a mental health professional requests that the Stephen Ministry caring relationship close, it may need to end immediately, or there may be an opportunity for the Stephen Minister to taper off the relationship over a designated period of time.[1] Again, the decision is up to the mental health professional. Whatever the case, the Stephen Minister should clearly communicate with the care receiver about what is happening. By doing so, the Stephen Minister will help facilitate the transition to professional care and help the caring relationship end on a positive note.

After a Referral to a Mental Health Professional Has Been Made

Communicating Key Information to a Care Receiver's Mental Health Professional

Mental health professionals to whom Stephen Ministry care receivers are referred need to know certain information about Stephen Ministry and the caring relationship. What a professional already knows may vary, so Stephen Ministers work together with the care receiver and Stephen Leaders to fill in any gaps and ensure the mental health professional knows all necessary information.

There are two kinds of information that mental health professionals need to know:

- **The existence of the caring relationship.** The care receiver's mental health professional needs to be aware that the care receiver also has a Stephen Minister. Because the care receiver makes the initial contact with the mental health professional's office, the care receiver is usually the one who will let the professional know about the caring relationship. This typically happens during the first meeting, when many mental health professionals gather a variety of information from new clients, including whether the person is receiving care from anyone else.

It is always necessary for a care receiver to let his or her mental health professional know about the Stephen Ministry caring relationship. In order to provide the best care, the mental health professional needs to have a complete and accurate picture of the care receiver's existing support systems. After the care receiver has met with the mental health professional, the Stephen Minister should check with the care receiver to verify that the mental health professional is aware of the caring relationship. If a care receiver does not inform the mental health professional about the caring relationship, the Stephen Minister should encourage the care receiver to do so. Should the care receiver refuse to tell the professional, then the Stephen Minister, in consultation with his or her Stephen Leaders, will need to bring the caring relationship to a close.

- **Details about Stephen Ministry.** So they can make the best decisions regarding Stephen Ministry, it's also important for mental health professionals to have a clear understanding of what Stephen Ministry is, how it works, and the kind of care that people receive through it. This includes the training Stephen Ministers go through, the kinds of care Stephen Ministers do and do not offer, and the supervision Stephen Ministers receive.

Generally, a Stephen Leader will provide this kind of foundational information to any mental health professional the congregation's Stephen Ministry has a relationship with, giving them a good understanding of what Stephen Ministry is before a care receiver is ever referred to that professional. If a care receiver is referred to a mental health professional who is not already familiar with Stephen Ministry, then the care receiver is typically the one to convey the information, using resources provided by Stephen Leaders.

See appendix B, "Key Information for Mental Health Professionals to Know about Stephen Ministry," for more about what mental health professionals need to know. Stephen Leaders also have resources available to help inform mental health professionals about Stephen Ministry.

Confidentiality and Privacy in Communications with a Mental Health Professional

Sometimes Stephen Ministers wonder how much, if any, communication they should have with a care receiver's mental health professional after a referral has been made. Overall, Stephen Ministers should follow the same guidelines for maintaining confidentiality with their care receiver's mental health professional as they would with anyone else.[2] In other words, with the exception of emergency situations where someone's safety is at risk, Stephen Ministers do not reveal information about their caring relationship to anyone else—including the mental health professional—without asking the care receiver's permission first.

Mental health professionals, for their part, have professional, ethical, and legal obligations to maintain the privacy of their clients. In the United States, the primary law that governs mental health professionals' responsibilities in this area is the Privacy Rule of the Health Insurance Portability and Accountability Act (HIPAA). This law provides guidelines about and places limitations on mental health care providers' ability to disclose information about clients without first obtaining written authorization from that client, including that a mental health professional cannot confirm or deny that a specific person is a client, disclose any information about conversations with a client, or discuss a client's situation with others. In some states, there are additional laws that further limit what information mental health professionals can share, how, and with whom.

In practice, this means that communication from a mental health professional to a Stephen Minister about a care receiver will usually happen with the care receiver acting as an intermediary. Part of the information mental health professionals receive about Stephen Ministry lets them know that, should they need to communicate to the Stephen Minister, they can do so by giving a written note to the care receiver to pass along.

Infrequently, a mental health professional may decide that it would be beneficial to speak directly with the Stephen Minister. In such situations, the Stephen Minister should defer to the mental health professional's instructions and guidance. The main responsibility for the Stephen Minister is to check that the care receiver is informed about what is happening. This is usually not an issue since the mental health professional will have already obtained the care receiver's permission to conduct such a conversation, and the care receiver may even be part of the discussion. Even so, it's good for Stephen Ministers to make sure the care receiver is fully aware of the meeting to prevent any problems.

Providing Care Concurrently with a Mental Health Professional

As mentioned previously, a mental health professional might decide that it's beneficial for the care receiver to continue meeting with his or her Stephen Minister in addition to receiving professional care. Here are a couple of points to help Stephen Ministers provide care concurrently with a mental health professional:

- **Have a clear understanding of the Stephen Minister's role.** Chapters 2–4 discussed in depth the role of the Stephen Minister, including the kinds of care Stephen Ministers do and do not provide. Mental health professionals are informed about the nature and boundaries of Stephen Ministry, meaning that permission for concurrent care is given with the expectation that Stephen Ministers will only provide care within the scope of their ministry as lay caregivers. Because of this, being fully aware of and staying within the bounds of the Stephen

Minister's role is a key way to most effectively support a care receiver who is getting professional help and avoid potentially interfering with the professional's care.

- **Remember that the mental health professional's expertise takes precedence.** Even when a mental health professional has given permission for the Stephen Ministry caring relationship to continue, Stephen Ministers need to keep in mind that the professional is the care receiver's primary caregiver. Recommendations, instructions, or decisions from the mental health professional should be followed by the care receiver and Stephen Minister. This also means that should the mental health professional determine that it would be best for the care receiver to stop seeing the Stephen Minister, the Stephen Minister should abide by that decision.

Although relatively simple, following these guidelines allows Stephen Ministers to be an effective complement to the mental health professional's care. Here's what one Stephen Minister shared about his experience providing care concurrently with his care receiver's counselor:

> "I learned that I had to let the counselor do his job. At first, I was always saying to myself, 'Why isn't the counselor doing this? Why isn't the counselor doing that?' I had to learn to really step back and let the counselor do his work, keeping the role of the Stephen Minister in

its place. With the counselor's expertise and training, he was able to help my care receiver to dig into things I couldn't get into. I just had to sit back and let the process flow—and after about a year or so of counseling, my care receiver had a big breakthrough."

Stephen Ministers should also remember that a mental health professional who gives permission for the Stephen Ministry caring relationship to continue does so when it is best for the care receiver's well-being. By caring concurrently with a mental health professional in accordance with these guidelines, Stephen Ministers have the opportunity to contribute to the care receiver getting the best care possible.

When a Care Receiver Has a Mental Health Professional at the Start of a Caring Relationship

This chapter has focused on situations in which a care receiver has been referred to a mental health professional through Stephen Ministry. One other situation to be aware of is when a Stephen Minister is assigned to a care receiver who is already seeing a mental health professional. Before making a connection like this, Stephen Leaders will have conducted a thorough preparation interview with the care receiver to make sure his or her needs are appropriate for

Stephen Ministry. They will also have already worked with the person to communicate about Stephen Ministry with his or her mental health professional and obtain permission from that professional for a Stephen Ministry caring relationship to begin.

Once such a caring relationship begins, it's a good idea for the Stephen Minister to find out a little from the care receiver about the professional care he or she is already receiving. This will give the Stephen Minister an idea of what the care receiver is working on with the mental health professional so that he or she has a better understanding of the overall context of the care receiver's needs and care. The Stephen Minister will also want to be sure to follow the principles described in this chapter about providing care concurrently with a mental health professional. Beyond that, the caring relationship can continue like normal, with the Stephen Minister providing Christ-centered emotional and spiritual support for as long as the care receiver needs it.

SOME FINAL THOUGHTS ON STEPHEN MINISTRY AND MENTAL HEALTH CARE

Although the vast majority of Stephen Ministry caring relationships never require a referral to a mental health professional, knowing how to recognize and respond to those situations that do is an important skill for every Stephen Minister. By having a firm grasp of the signs that a care receiver's needs may be outside the boundaries of Stephen Ministry, Stephen Ministers can preserve the quality of their own caregiving and ensure that care receivers get the most appropriate type and level of care. With the knowledge and skills from their training at their disposal, Stephen Ministers can have confidence in their ability to respond effectively if mental health issues come up in a caring relationship.

This chapter highlights some concluding thoughts for Stephen Ministers to reflect on throughout their training and caring. These points all serve to prepare Stephen Ministers for their ministry and illustrate the value of the care they offer, particularly in the area of mental health.

Stephen Ministry within the Broader Context of Mental Health Care

This book has focused on how Stephen Ministers can help care receivers who are dealing with mental health issues, especially those outside the boundaries of Stephen Ministry. Within those boundaries, however, Stephen Ministers' care can have a strong positive impact on the overall mental health of care receivers, whether professional care is required or not. Although Stephen Ministry is not professional mental health care, it *is* care that can do a lot to help a person's mental health. As one marriage and family therapist put it, "Stephen Ministers instill a sense of hope in their care receivers and help them recognize that they are not alone. The consistency of their love, nonjudgmental attitude, and support is so valuable."

Just like our physical health, our mental health is important to our overall well-being. While mental health care is often thought of only as treatment for serious issues, in reality it encompasses a much broader range of activities. The chart on the next page shows how mental health care parallels physical health care in three areas: maintenance of good health, prevention of health crises, and health crisis intervention.

Some Final Thoughts on Stephen Ministry and Mental Health

	Physical Health Care	Mental Health Care
Maintenance of Good Health	• Staying active • Exercising regularly • Maintaining a good sleep routine • Eating healthy foods	• Having solid social and spiritual support systems • Developing and using healthy ways of coping with life challenges
Prevention of Health Crises	• Stretching before exercise • Washing hands regularly • Having regular checkups with a physician	• Talking with others about life challenges or difficult emotions • Having a Stephen Minister during a difficult life situation
Health Crisis Intervention	• Going to urgent care or the emergency room • Having surgery • Going through physical therapy after an injury	• Seeing a mental health professional* • Going through a rehabilitation program

* *Mental health professionals can also operate in the areas of maintenance and prevention.*

As the chart illustrates, Stephen Ministers can play a valuable role in caring for people's mental health. A chaplain and counselor who serves as a Stephen Leader said, "When people are going through some kind of difficult situation and have someone—like a Stephen Minister—walking alongside them, it can help prevent more serious mental health issues down the road." In addition to prevention of health crises, Stephen Ministers also frequently help in the area of maintenance, providing support that helps people preserve their mental well-being in the midst of difficult situations.

Previous chapters have described how a person's psychological needs may sometimes be greater than what a Stephen Minister is equipped to handle; for example, when a person is experiencing a mental health crisis like severe depression or suicidal ideation. That's when a mental health professional should be involved to intervene. In most caring relationships, though, Stephen Ministry is a highly effective source of emotional and spiritual support, caring for the whole person and providing a deep level of comfort and solace.

Understanding and Addressing the Mental Health Stigma

Although public awareness about mental health issues and care continues to improve, the topic is still often surrounded by a stigma. As a result, some people—including both Stephen Ministers and care receivers—may be uncomfortable talking about mental health. It's important for Stephen Ministers to be aware of this challenge so that they can be aware of the concerns and feelings care receivers may have and communicate in ways that can help counteract the stigma.

Dr. Patrick Corrigan, a professor of psychology and researcher, identifies two main forms of mental health stigma: public stigma and self-stigma. Public stigma involves societal stereotypes, prejudices, and the discrimination individuals with mental health issues often face, while self-stigma occurs when a person internalizes society's negative messages about mental health and applies them personally.[1] Both issues are closely linked, as societal factors like everyday language ("Are you insane?"), unfavorable or sensationalized media depictions of mental health issues, and experiences of discrimination can cause individuals to apply negative beliefs to themselves.[2]

The mental health stigma in both of these forms can have many harmful effects. An international team of researchers identified many concerns that individuals with mental health issues may have as a result of the stigma, such as the fear of social judgment or rejection, being labeled as mentally ill, or being blamed for their condition. They may feel shame or embarrassment, see themselves as weak or having failed at dealing with life's problems, or believe they are "not normal" and will never recover.[3] Probably the most harmful effect, though, is when the stigma discourages people from talking about or seeking help for mental health issues.

As caregivers who may encounter individuals with mental health issues, Stephen Ministers need to be aware of the stigma associated with mental disorders and receiving treatment for them—and how it can affect the ways both care receivers and Stephen Ministers communicate about the topic. Fortunately, many of the caring skills that are foundational to Stephen Ministry—listening, validation, providing a nonjudgmental presence, to name a few—can help counteract these challenges. Even so, Stephen Ministers should take particular care to avoid unintentionally reinforcing the stigma, particularly when a care receiver may need professional care. As one psychologist said, "Some care receivers may feel that it is embarrassing to see a mental health professional, so Stephen Ministers should approach any discussion of a referral with knowledge, compassion, and understanding."

The mental health stigma is an unfortunate reality, but in the context of a one-to-one caring relationship Stephen Ministers have a unique opportunity to address its harmful effects. The personal, trusting relationship between a Stephen Minister and a care receiver is a powerful vehicle for encouraging a more positive perspective on mental health care. By emphasizing the value of professional care, normalizing a care receiver's needs, and consistently demonstrating concern and acceptance, Stephen Ministers can overcome

Some Final Thoughts on Stephen Ministry and Mental Health

the problems caused by the mental health stigma, empowering care receivers to seek the care they need.

Trusting Your Training and Resources

Stephen Ministers are very well trained when it comes to the boundaries, signs, and steps related to responding to mental health issues. While they may understandably feel a bit nervous when they encounter a possible need for a referral, they can trust their training and resources to guide them through the process. Here's what a Stephen Minister shared about her experience of referring a care receiver with depression to a mental health professional:

> "Trust your training. Stephen Minister training gives you great tools, and you can believe in the quality of the training you've received. That's what's going to guide you through these situations."

Stephen Ministers regularly find that, in the moment when a possible mental health issue surfaces in a caring relationship, their training kicks in, with key points from their reading and skill practices coming back to them at just the right time. The two main steps of their response—*recognizing* signs of a possible issue and working with others to *refer*—are activities Stephen Ministers are fully capable of accomplishing. With those steps in mind, the rest of the process and details will fall naturally into place.

Stephen Ministers should also remember that the resources they received in training are always available and can continue to serve them long after training has ended and their first caring relationships have started. In particular, this book is a valuable ongoing guide and reference—any time a mental health situation comes up, Stephen Ministers can return to these pages for guidance.

On the Same Team

Along with their training and resources, Stephen Ministers can also rely on the support of others when potential mental health issues arise in a caring relationship. Supervision Groups, Stephen Leaders (particularly the Community Resource Contacts), and pastors are all available for Stephen Ministers, ensuring that they never have to navigate these situations on their own. Stephen Ministers can take comfort in knowing that everyone on the Stephen Ministry team has the same goal of getting the care receiver the best care possible.

In addition, it's important to remember that the mental health professionals who provide care to care receivers share that goal too. Regardless of what happens with a caring relationship—whether concurrent care with a professional or closure—Stephen Ministers can have confidence that mental health professionals are just as committed to improving care receivers' health and preserving their well-being. Here's what one social worker said:

"Mental health professionals care about care receivers and want them to know they are cared for and heard, just like Stephen Ministers do. Stephen Ministers and mental health professionals are all working together for the same outcome: for the care receiver's suffering to be minimized and health to be restored."

This consistent desire for the good of the care receiver is a powerful unifying factor that draws caregivers together. Ultimately, everyone is on the same team.

Fulfilling the Purpose of Stephen Ministry

A central theme of this book is that connecting a care receiver with a mental health professional fulfills the purpose of Stephen Ministry by helping that individual get the best care possible. A care receiver being able to say something like, "Thanks to my Stephen Minister, I started seeing a counselor, and it made a big difference for me," is a wonderful thing. The same is true when a Stephen Ministry caring relationship helps a care receiver avoid a mental health crisis that would require professional care. When a hurting person gets the appropriate type and level of care for his or her needs, it's good for the care receiver, good for the Stephen Minister, and good for the congregation and its ministry.

As a Stephen Minister, you are a lay Christian caregiver who is trained, commissioned, and supervised in your ministry to bring God's healing love to those who are broken and suffering, including those who may face the difficulties that come with mental health issues. In all your caring relationships, you can take comfort and confidence in the fact that no matter what challenges you or your care receiver may encounter, God is always with you.

APPENDIX A

WHAT TO SAY—AND WHAT NOT TO SAY—WHEN REFERRING A CARE RECEIVER TO A MENTAL HEALTH PROFESSIONAL

As discussed in chapter 7, there are six steps for conducting a conversation about a mental health referral with a care receiver:

1. Pray for God's guidance and help.
2. Think about what to say ahead of time.

Prior to the caring visit.

3. Express care and concern for the care receiver.
4. Make the recommendation.
5. Listen to the care receiver's response.
6. Assertively help the care receiver commit to connecting with a mental health professional.

During the caring visit.

This appendix is a tool for Stephen Ministers who are preparing to talk with a care receiver about a referral to a mental health professional, providing practical guidelines and examples for carrying out this conversation during the caring visit with a focus on steps 3, 4, 5, and 6.

What to Say during a Conversation about a Mental Health Referral

The sections that follow provide sample conversations and suggested wording for each step in suggesting a mental health referral. They can serve as a guide when you're preparing to talk with a care receiver about a referral and planning what you might say. Specific wording is highlighted in each section's example dialogue and then explained in the paragraphs that follow.

> **Note:** The examples in the following sections use the term *mental health professional* as a general placeholder, but depending on the specifics of the situation you might use another term, such as *counselor* or *therapist*.

Express Care and Concern for the Care Receiver

Begin by assuring the care receiver that you care for and are concerned about him or her. Doing so establishes a positive, warm tone for the conversation and paves the way for the person to be receptive to a referral to a mental health professional. Here's an example of how a Stephen Minister might broach the topic of a referral:

Stephen Minister: . . . So, ① I know things have been really tough for you, especially lately. And because ② it's important to me that you get the right kind of care, I've been thinking about how that can happen. . . .

There are two points to note here. First ①, the Stephen Minister reflects content discussed in prior conversations, saying, "I know things have been really tough for you, especially lately." This kind of reflection communicates care in a powerful way because it lets the care receiver know that the Stephen Minister has truly been listening.

Second ②, the Stephen Minister states, "It's important to me that you get the right kind of care." A statement like this clearly expresses the Stephen Minister's sincere interest in the care receiver's well-being and so paves the way for the next step of the conversation.

As the example shows, it's not necessary to say a lot during this step. In fact, it's usually best to be brief so as not to create anxiety about what you're going to say next. Once you've let your care receiver know that you genuinely care about him or her, move on to the next step.

Here are a couple of other examples of how you might express care and concern:

- "You said the last time we met that you feel like you're not making any progress toward 'getting over this setback' in your life. I know it took a lot of courage for you to share that, and I really want to be a support for you as you're working through things."

- "As we've been meeting, we've talked about how you've felt very depressed. You're important to me, and I want you to have the help you need to get through this."

Make the Recommendation

Shortly after expressing your care and concern, you'll want to make your recommendation that the care receiver meet with a mental health professional. Here's how the Stephen Minister from the previous section might continue the conversation:

Stephen Minister: I've been thinking about how that can happen. With everything you're going through, ① I think it would be really good for you to talk with a mental health professional.

Care Receiver: I wondered if you were going to say something like that. I've thought about getting a counselor before, but I wasn't sure it would help. You think I should?

Stephen Minister: Yes, I do. ② You told me last week that your anxiety has been so bad that you can't focus at work, and a mental health professional would be the best person to help you with that kind of challenge. ③ As a Stephen Minister, I've gone through a lot of training, but I'm not an expert in this area. Like I said before, I want you to have the best care possible, and right now,

Appendix A

that means getting you connected with a mental health professional. . . ."

The clarity and assertiveness of the ❶ first highlighted phrase make it highly effective. It leaves no room for misunderstanding about what you're recommending, and it communicates a strong belief that receiving professional care is in the care receiver's best interest. Make your own initial recommendation similarly simple and straightforward.

The ❷ second highlighted phrase is another illustration of the importance of reflection in this kind of conversation. By mentioning what the care receiver has said, you can help the care receiver gain new perspective, drawing a clear connection between his or her experiences and a need for professional care.

The ❸ third phrase, mentioning the limitations of the Stephen Minister's role, is helpful because it provides a reason for the referral that isn't directly related to the care receiver. By taking some of the focus off the person and his or her needs and placing it on the boundaries of your care as a Stephen Minister, you can help alleviate potential defensiveness from the care receiver.

Here are a couple of other examples of how you might make the recommendation that a care receiver connect with a mental health professional:

- "I'd like to help you connect with a mental health professional."

- "I really believe a mental health professional would best be able to meet your needs."

Listen to the Care Receiver's Response

Once you've made your initial recommendation and explained your reasons for suggesting a mental health professional, give the care receiver an opportunity to share any thoughts and feelings about the referral. Here's how the conversation might continue:

Stephen Minister: . . . I want you to have the best care possible, and right now that means getting you connected with a mental health professional. *(Brief pause)* 1 What are you thinking right now?

Care Receiver: Well, I don't really like the idea of it, if I'm being honest. I mean, my anxiety has been really bad lately, but I just don't know if seeing a therapist would really even help. I had a friend in college who had a counselor, but he was really depressed—even suicidal sometimes. I'm not like that.

Stephen Minister: 2 You just said that you don't really like the idea of seeing a therapist. Tell me more about that.

Care Receiver: I guess it's just that I've always thought of seeing a counselor as sort of like, I don't know… admitting defeat? Like I couldn't pull myself together on my own. So that's part of it. But also, I'm already meeting with you. Do you think getting a therapist would make that much of a difference?

Stephen Minister: I really think it would. These professionals are specifically trained to help with challenges like what you're experiencing. The ones on that list I gave you have met with our Stephen Leaders, and we know they're very good. ③ I'm sure they would be helpful for you. . . .

The ① first two highlighted phrases are good examples of how you might invite a care receiver to share thoughts and feelings after making your recommendation. In particular, with ② the second phrase the Stephen Minister is reflecting some of what the care receiver has just said, which leads naturally into another invitation for the care receiver to share. The Stephen Minister doesn't rush to respond to the care receiver's statements, instead asking the care receiver to explore a specific thought in more depth first.

A key part of the Stephen Minister's response is in the ③ third highlighted phrase, where the Stephen Minister states confidently that the referral would help the care receiver. As you listen to the care receiver and invite sharing, your positive and confident communication about the referral is an effective way to help the care receiver become more receptive to the idea.

Care receivers may have a variety of reactions to the recommendation of a referral, from immediate interest to uncertainty to strong reluctance. They may need to get those thoughts and feelings out before they're ready to consider their options. Whatever way the care receiver responds, you'll still go through the same process of using your Stephen Ministry skills to listen, affirm, reflect, and validate—all while remaining positive about the referral's benefits for the care receiver.

Assertively Help the Care Receiver Commit to Connecting with a Mental Health Professional

After listening to any thoughts, feelings, or concerns the care receiver has, the final step is to assertively encourage the care receiver to commit to contacting a mental health professional. Here's how the Stephen Minister in the example might handle this final step:

Stephen Minister: . . . I'm sure they would make a difference for you.

Care Receiver: I want to believe that. I really do. It's just hard. (Pause) Sorry, I don't mean to get emotional on you.

Stephen Minister: You don't have to apologize. I can tell this isn't easy for you.

Care Receiver: Thanks. . . . Well, since it's you saying this, I guess it is probably a good idea.

Stephen Minister: I'm glad to hear you say that. I've put together a short list of some professionals our Stephen Ministry team has identified. *(Hands list to care receiver)* I wanted you to have a few options to consider. ❶ You can take some time to look over the information and decide which one to call. It's very important to me that you get the right kind of care, so ❷ will you commit to contacting one of these mental health professionals?

Care Receiver: (Pause) Okay. I'll look over the stuff you gave me and give one of them a call.

Stephen Minister: That's great. ❸ I'll call you in a couple of days to see how it goes.

The ❶ first highlighted sentence builds effectively on the care receiver's expression of openness to getting in touch with a mental health professional. Assuring the care receiver that immediate action isn't needed takes some of the pressure off the person, which can help avoid knee-jerk reactions. As noted in chapter 7, it's vital that a care receiver take ownership of the decision. Letting the care receiver know that there's time to think through the process reduces the chances of a halfhearted yes simply to satisfy the Stephen Minister, only for the care receiver to later decide against making the contact.

The ❷ second highlight is another example of the importance of being both gentle and direct during these conversations. Using a simple, closed-ended question, the Stephen Minister assertively asks for the care receiver's commitment to getting the needed care, without excessive pressure. This paves the way for the care receiver to agree.

Finally, the ❸ third highlighted phrase lets the care receiver know that the Stephen Minister will be checking in later specifically about the referral. This is important so that the care receiver isn't surprised by the follow-up and doesn't assume it's because of a lack of trust on the Stephen Minister's part. Also, note that the Stephen Minister talks about following up about how the call went—not whether the care receiver followed through. This communicates the Stephen Minister's confidence that the care receiver will take action in a positive, supportive way, without inducing a sense of obligation or guilt.

Here are a couple of other examples of what you might say to assertively help a care receiver commit to contacting a mental health professional:

- "I really believe the care of a mental health professional is what you need right now, so I'd like you to get in touch and meet with one."

- "It's good to hear you're open to meeting with a mental health professional. The next step is for you to contact one and have an initial meeting."

What *Not* to Say during a Referral Conversation

Along with knowing what to say during a referral conversation, it's important to know what not to say, in order to avoid inadvertently creating barriers to a care receiver's willingness to receive professional care.

Emotionally Charged Language

When a Stephen Minister and care receiver are talking about a referral to a mental health professional, it's natural for both to experience some heightened emotions. To help keep those emotions at a manageable level, the Stephen Minister will want to avoid emotionally-charged language that might offend, frighten, or otherwise upset a care receiver. Here are some examples:

- "It's obvious that things are getting worse, and if you don't get help soon, who knows what could happen to you!"

- "You have to get a therapist. I'm so worried about you that I can hardly think straight."

- "I talked about you with my Supervision Group and all my Stephen Leaders, and we're all in agreement you need way more help than a Stephen Minister can provide."

Judgments or Evaluations

The social stigma around mental health issues and other factors may cause a care receiver to react defensively to a recommendation of a referral to a mental health professional. Language that the care receiver might perceive as judgmental or diagnostic can generate greater defensiveness, causing the person to be much less open to the referral. Here are some examples:

- "You've been grieving for a lot longer than you should. You should think about getting professional help so you can stop being so sad all the time."

- "Most people would have adapted to all this by now. You need to see a counselor."

- "If you can't just get over being depressed, I think you should get a therapist."

Jargon

It's best not to use any jargon related to the area of mental health, especially anything that might be interpreted as a diagnosis of a mental disorder. If the care receiver doesn't understand the terminology being used, or if it sounds like a formal diagnosis of some kind, it's likely to raise his or her level of anxiety. Here are some types of jargon to avoid:

- Names of specific mental disorders or technical descriptions of symptoms

- In-depth details about or descriptions of the types of mental health professionals, their qualifications, or related organizations

- Terminology related to treatment methods

- Acronyms or abbreviations for any terms used in the mental health field

Anything Potentially Guilt-Inducing

For a referral conversation to be successful, it's crucial that the care receiver take responsibility for the decision to meet with a mental health professional. Using words that might push a care receiver to agree to see a mental health professional out of guilt runs directly counter to this goal. A care receiver who agrees to connect with a professional out of guilt is unlikely to be fully invested in the process of healing. Here are some examples of statements that might induce guilt:

- "If you won't do it for yourself, do it for me."

- "If you don't get help, you're basically saying you don't want to get better."

- "Your family is really worried. You owe it to them to get help."

WHEN AND HOW TO USE MENTAL HEALTH RESOURCES

Overall, remaining non-anxious and communicating in a caring, assertive way will go a long way toward helping your care receiver make and take ownership of the decision to contact a mental health professional. Your recommendation of professional help may be just what a care receiver needs to start moving toward getting the care he or she needs. Be confident that having this conversation is in the care receiver's best interests, and remember that God will be there to guide you as you refer your care receiver to a mental health professional.

APPENDIX B

KEY INFORMATION FOR MENTAL HEALTH PROFESSIONALS TO KNOW ABOUT STEPHEN MINISTRY

Mental health professionals who work with Stephen Ministry care receivers need to have a clear picture of what Stephen Ministry is, how it works, and the kind of care a Stephen Minister provides. It's helpful for Stephen Ministers to be aware of what information is shared with mental health professionals, particularly so that they're on the same page if they end up caring for a person concurrently with a mental health professional.

What Do Mental Health Professionals Need to Know about Stephen Ministry?

Mental health professionals need to be familiar with two main categories of information about Stephen Ministry:

1) what Stephen Ministry is and how it works; and

2) the kinds of care Stephen Ministers provide.

The following information is taken from a *Stephen Ministry Leader's Manual* document that Stephen Leaders share with mental health professionals who may receive care receiver referrals.

1. What Is Stephen Ministry, and How Does It Work?

Stephen Ministry is a system that congregations use to organize, train, and supervise a team of lay caregivers—called Stephen Ministers—to provide one-to-one, confidential, Christian care to people who are hurting.

Stephen Ministry began in 1975, when Rev. Kenneth C. Haugk, Ph.D., a clinical psychologist and pastor in St. Louis, Missouri, realized that the needs for care in his congregation were more than he could meet alone. Drawing on his education and experience in both psychology and theology to train nine church members as the first Stephen Ministers, he equipped them to provide pastoral care to people going through difficult times in life. The ministry was so effective that those Stephen Ministers encouraged Dr. Haugk to share it with other congregations.

Recognizing the broader need for this kind of care, Dr. Haugk founded Stephen Ministries St. Louis, a Christian educational not-for-profit organization, to help bring Stephen Ministry to other congregations. Today, thousands of congregations and other organizations around the world use Stephen Ministry to equip laypeople to provide high-quality emotional and spiritual care to individuals going through difficult times in life.

This graphic shows the overall structure of Stephen Ministry and how the system works.

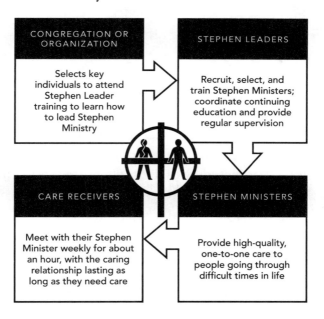

When beginning Stephen Ministry, a congregation or organization selects a few key individuals—including pastors, staff, and lay leaders—to attend a one-week training course where they are trained as *Stephen Leaders*. These leaders return home to begin and direct Stephen Ministry, which includes interviewing and selecting laypeople to serve as *Stephen Ministers* and providing them with 50 hours of caring ministry training using material provided by Stephen Ministries. Once Stephen Ministers have completed this initial training, Stephen Leaders match them with *care receivers*—individuals who are going through difficult times in life.

Stephen Ministers typically have one care receiver at a time and meet with that person once a week for about an hour. These *caring relationships* last for as long as the person's need for care persists. Once a caring relationship has ended, a Stephen Minister can be assigned a new care receiver. Stephen Ministers also participate in twice monthly continuing education and small group peer supervision coordinated by their Stephen Leaders to ensure that they receive the support, guidance, and accountability they need for effective caring.

2. What Kind of Care Do Stephen Ministers Provide?

Stephen Ministers are trained lay caregivers who provide one-to-one, confidential Christian care. Following are explanations of the key elements of this description:

- **Lay:** Stephen Ministers are not professional caregivers; they are well-trained and supervised volunteers who provide a high level of care. Their role is fundamentally different from that of a counselor, therapist, or pastor. When a care receiver has need for care beyond what a Stephen Minister is trained to provide, the Stephen Minister consults with a Stephen Leader or pastor to connect the care receiver with the appropriate type and level of care, such as professional mental health care.

- **One-to-one:** Each Stephen Minister is matched with one care receiver of the same gender. The two meet in person, typically once a week for about an hour, in a mutually agreed-upon setting.

- **Confidential:** Stephen Ministers maintain confidentiality about care receivers' identities and personal information. In situations where there's a risk of harm to the care receiver or others, Stephen Ministers are trained to appropriately widen the circle of confidentiality to include emergency services, Stephen Ministry leadership, mental health professionals, and others who can provide the level of help the person needs.

- **Christian:** Stephen Ministers are motivated to care by their Christian faith. When it comes to spiritual matters, though, Stephen Ministers meet their care receivers where they are, helping them work through life challenges without pressuring them or forcing faith on them.

- **Care:** Stephen Ministers care by providing emotional and spiritual support—listening, supporting, and helping their care receivers explore feelings without being judgmental. Their role does not include providing other types of assistance such as shopping, transportation, or childcare, although at times they may help care receivers identify ways to fill those needs. An important part of Stephen Ministers' training involves learning how to establish and maintain appropriate boundaries with care receivers, which equips them to provide the best possible care within the scope of their abilities as lay caregivers.

Stephen Ministers are equipped to provide care in a wide variety of situations. Some of the most common needs for which Stephen Ministers provide care are shown here.

- Grief
- Relocation or other life transitions
- Divorce
- Caregiver for a love one
- Health issues
- Infertility, miscarriage, and related crises
- Spiritual crisis
- Terminal illness/end of life issues
- Job loss/financial difficulties
- A variety of other life challenges

The careful development of the Stephen Ministry system and the clearly defined role of the Stephen Minister have been foundational to the ministry's success over the years. Since 1975, hundreds of thousands of people have been trained as Stephen Ministers, and they have gone on to provide excellent, much-needed care to millions of people worldwide.

APPENDIX C

GUIDELINES FOR MENTAL HEALTH PROFESSIONALS SERVING AS STEPHEN MINISTERS

Over the years, many mental health professionals have been trained and served as Stephen Ministers, seeing it as an opportunity to be involved in providing distinctively Christ-centered care to hurting people. Here's what one mental health professional said about his experience:

> "Being a Stephen Minister has truly enriched my life. The training has given me new skills in addition to the ones I've gained through my professional career, and serving has helped me better understand myself and be more aware of and able to express my own emotions. Most importantly, it's a way to keep Christ at the forefront of my life."

This is just one example of how mental health professionals have experienced personal growth, deepened their faith, and found a meaningful, fulfilling way to serve through Stephen Ministry.

When mental health professionals are trained as Stephen Ministers, they often have questions about how they can or should use their professional knowledge and skills in this lay ministry role, as well as about any legal considerations they should be aware of. This appendix provides guidelines and suggestions for how mental health professionals can avoid potential pitfalls and provide quality care while serving as Stephen Ministers.

Maintain Clear Boundaries

One of the most important guidelines is to maintain clear boundaries between your roles as a Stephen Minister and as a mental health professional. When you meet with your care receiver as a Stephen Minister, you provide the care of a Stephen Minister—not any other kind of care. Chapters 2–4 say more about the kinds of care Stephen Ministers do and do not provide.

When you arrive for a caring visit, you'll leave at the door any methods or techniques that are unique to your profession. Instead, you'll make use of the tools of your Stephen Minister training—such as active listening, recognizing and responding to feelings, validation, the ministry of presence, affirmation, and distinctively Christian resources—while walking alongside your care receiver. This doesn't mean you can't use any of your professional skills in a Stephen Ministry caring relationship, but before doing so, ask yourself whether using those skills would go beyond the care of a Stephen Minister or blur the boundary between providing lay care and professional care. When in doubt, err on the side of sticking with your Stephen Ministry skills.

Appendix C

Downplay Your Profession to Care Receivers

One effective way to help establish and maintain clear boundaries is to downplay your profession with your care receiver. This doesn't mean you should hide or be untruthful about your profession—rather, if asked what you do for a living, simply and briefly share that you're a mental health professional and then move on. It's also good to clearly state to the care receiver that you're there to provide care only as a Stephen Minister and not in a professional capacity. Here's an example of what that might look like:

Care Receiver: . . . so, I've been working at that same company for almost twenty years now—I can't believe it's been that long, honestly. What do you do for a living?

Stephen Minister: I actually have a private practice as a psychologist. I started it a few years back after working in a hospital setting for several years.

Care Receiver: A psychologist, huh? And you're also a Stephen Minister?

Stephen Minister: That's right. I really felt called to this ministry. I want to be clear, though, that when I meet with you, I'm not doing so as a therapist or a counselor or anything like that. I'm here to care for you as a Stephen Minister, not as a psychologist.

Care Receiver: Sure, that makes sense.

Stephen Minister: So, you were saying earlier that you've been having a hard time since your father passed away. Tell me more about that.

By briefly acknowledging your profession without dwelling on it and by clearly communicating that you are there only as a Stephen Minister, you set appropriate expectations for the caring relationship up front.

Also, if the care receiver doesn't ask what you do professionally, there's no need to bring it up unless you feel more comfortable doing so up front. Either way, what you do as a Stephen Minister won't change—you can just go ahead and provide high-quality Stephen Ministry care as you've been trained to do.

When Necessary, Consult with Others and Make a Referral

As a mental health professional, you are particularly well equipped to recognize when a care receiver may need care beyond what a Stephen Minister can offer. You certainly can make use of your professional knowledge of the signs and symptoms of various mental disorders to determine if a referral is needed. Before acting on that knowledge, however, it's important to consult with your Stephen Leaders and work the process described in chapter 7, "How to Refer a Care Receiver to a Mental Health Professional." Even if your professional knowledge makes a care receiver's needs obvious to you, it's still crucial that you follow the Stephen Ministry process of making referrals in consultation with others so that the leadership responsible for oversight of Stephen Ministry is aware of the situation.

To avoid potential conflicts of interest, you should not allow your current or former care receivers to be connected with you in a professional capacity. Such a connection would raise ethical concerns and blur the line between your role as the person's Stephen Minister and as a mental health professional, even if the person stops being your Stephen Ministry care receiver and becomes a client instead. If your care receiver needs professional care, he or she should be referred to a mental health professional other than yourself.

Carefully Consider How You Use Your Professional Expertise

Be thoughtful about the ways you use your professional skills and insight in the context of Stephen Ministry. In your caring relationships, you'll want to use only those skills that are appropriate for a lay caregiver so that you don't cross over into giving professional care.

Likewise, in your Supervision Group, be intentional and focused in how you share your professional expertise with your fellow Stephen Ministers as lay caregivers, applying those insights only where it's relevant and appropriate to do so. You'll want to avoid an environment where others in your group always look to you for advice or defer to your thoughts and opinions. Stephen Minister training module 16, "Supervision: A Key to Quality Christian Care," emphasizes that supervision is a collaborative, process-focused meeting of a group of peers in caregiving. Much like a caring relationship between a Stephen Minister and care receiver, supervision is an opportunity for Stephen Ministers to express feelings and come up with their own answers to challenges they may be facing. It's important that your professional expertise contribute positively to that process and not disrupt it. As long as you follow the process of Stephen Ministry supervision, you shouldn't encounter any issues.

An Important Safeguard: Check with Insurance Providers

Finally, it's important to touch base with your congregation's insurance provider and your own professional insurance provider before taking on your first care receiver. In the United States, the Volunteer Protection Act of 1997 (VPA) provides a minimum level of protection for volunteers, including healthcare professionals who volunteer in their area of practice. However, individual states may have other laws that further limit a professional's liability or otherwise preempt the VPA.

Be sure to communicate in advance with insurance providers to make sure that you and your congregation have a clear understanding of applicable laws in your area. Doing so can make it clear whether your volunteering as a Stephen Minister is covered by your congregation's volunteer insurance, your own professional liability insurance, or both.

Because volunteering as a Stephen Minister involves filling a lay role—rather than using professional expertise in a volunteer context—mental health professionals who serve as Stephen Ministers may not need any extra insurance. That said, it's always best to check with insurance providers to minimize any possible risk for both you and for your congregation.

When checking with insurance providers, you may want to involve at least one of your Stephen Leaders, or possibly your pastor, in the conversation. These discussions don't need to be lengthy, but it's especially important to make two points clear for insurance providers:

- **The scope of your activities as a Stephen Minister.** Stephen Ministers provide one-to-one, confidential, Christian care that takes the form of emotional and spiritual support. Their care involves listening, reflecting a care receiver's thoughts and feelings, validating the care receiver's experiences, using distinctively Christian resources, and focusing on the process of caring. There are also clear boundaries around the types of care that Stephen Ministers provide—for instance, they don't give medical advice, and they refer care receivers to a mental health professional when necessary. Stephen Ministers are supervised in peer groups, and their ministry is overseen by Stephen Leaders.

- **The fact that, as a Stephen Minister, you are functioning solely in a lay capacity.** A defining aspect of a Stephen Minister's role is that they are lay caregivers who provide lay care. Although Stephen Ministers do receive training in various areas for their ministry, they are still volunteers who are not trained to provide any kind of professional care. Anyone who serves as a Stephen Minister, regardless of profession, functions in a lay role.

Chapters 2–4 of this book, "Defining the Stephen Minister's Role," "What Stephen Ministers Do," and "What Stephen Ministers Do Not Do," can be a useful resource to help communicate this information. By sharing what you will and will not be doing as a Stephen Minister and by making it clear that you are serving in a lay capacity using lay caregiving skills, not your professional skills, you'll help insurance providers understand the nature of your work as a Stephen Minister.

As mentioned at the beginning of this appendix, you are joining thousands of other mental health professionals who have become Stephen Ministers and served in this ministry successfully. Although you will need to be careful to maintain clear boundaries between your work as a Stephen

Appendix C

Minister and a mental health professional, following the guidance in this appendix will help you provide excellent care to your care receivers, avoid risks, and enjoy the fruits of serving in this ministry.

NOTES

CHAPTER 1

1 *Diagnostic and Statistical Manual of Mental Disorders*, 5th ed. (Arlington: American Psychiatric Association, 2013), p. 20.

CHAPTER 2

1 Kenneth C. Haugk, *Discovering God's Vision for Your Life: You and Your Spiritual Gifts, Ministry Mobilization Manual* (Saint Louis: Tebunah Ministries, 2015), p. 96.

2 Kenneth C. Haugk, *Don't Sing Songs to a Heavy Heart: How to Relate to Those Who Are Suffering* (Saint Louis: Stephen Ministries, 2004), p. 35.

CHAPTER 3

1 "Module 9: Confidentiality," *Stephen Minister Training Manual* (Saint Louis: Stephen Ministries, 2020), p. 176.

2 Kenneth C. Haugk, *Christian Caregiving—a Way of Life,* 2nd ed. (Saint Louis: Stephen Ministries, 2020), p. 109.

CHAPTER 5

1 Much of the information in this chapter applies specifically to professionals within the United States. For professionals outside the US, confirm what the local requirements and expectations are.

2 "Clinical Psychology," American Psychological Association, accessed November 26, 2019, https://www.apa.org/ed/graduate/specialize/clinical.

3 "Clinical Social Work," National Association of Social Workers, accessed November 26, 2019, https://www.socialworkers.org/Practice/Clinical-Social-Work.

4 "What is Counseling Psychology," Society of Counseling Psychology, Division 17, accessed November 26, 2019, https://www.div17.org/about-cp/what-is-counseling-psychology/.

5 Patricia R. Roger and Gerald Stone, "Counseling Psychology vs Clinical Psychology," Society of Counseling Psychology, Division 17, accessed November 26, 2019, https://www.div17.org/about-cp/counseling-vs-clinical-psychology/.

6 "Who Are Licensed Professional Counselors," American Counseling Association, accessed November 26, 2019, https://www.counseling.org/PublicPolicy/WhoAreLPCs.pdf, p. 1.

7 "About Marriage and Family Therapists," American Association for Marriage and Family Therapy, accessed November 26, 2019, https://www.aamft.org/About_AAMFT/About_Marriage_and_Family_Therapists.aspx.

8 "Psychiatric-Mental Health Nurses," American Psychiatric Nurses Association, accessed November 26, 2019, https://www.apna.org/i4a/pages/index.cfm?pageid=3292.

9 "What is Psychiatry?" American Psychiatric Association, accessed November 26, 2019, https://www.psychiatry.org/patients-families/what-is-psychiatry.

CHAPTER 6

1 David D. Burns, *Feeling Good: The New Mood Therapy* (New York: William Morrow and Company, Inc., 1980), p. 40–41.

2 Stephen Minister training module 9, "Confidentiality," provides a process for responding to emergency situations where someone's safety is at risk.

CHAPTER 7

1 Stephen Ministers learn more about when and how to use their Community Resource Contacts in Stephen Minister training module 11, "Using Mental Health Professionals and Other Community Resources."

2 Stephen Ministers learn about when and how to use their Stephen Ministry Crisis Contacts in Stephen Minister training module 9, "Confidentiality."

Notes

CHAPTER 8

1 Stephen Ministers learn the standard process for closing a caring relationship, including how to taper off visits, in Stephen Minister training module 15, "Bringing the Caring Relationship to a Close." Even when a caring relationship is ending abruptly due to a mental health referral, many of the principles discussed in that module still apply.

2 Stephen Minister training module 9, "Confidentiality," covers standard practices for maintaining confidentiality in Stephen Ministry caring relationships.

CHAPTER 9

1 Patrick Corrigan, "How Stigma Interferes with Mental Health Care," *American Psychologist* 59 (October 2004), pp. 616–618.

2 Andrew G. Martinez and Stephen P. Hinshaw, "Mental Health Stigma: Theory, Developmental Issues, and Research Priorities," *Developmental Psychopathy* (Hoboken, NJ: John Wiley & Sons, Inc., 2016), pp. 1014–1015.

3 S. Clement, et al., "What is the impact of mental health-related stigma on help-seeking? A systematic review of quantitative and qualitative studies," *Psychological Medicine* 45 (2015), accessed November 26, 2019, https://doi.org/10.1017/S0033291714000129.

ACKNOWLEDGMENTS

This second edition of *When and How to Use Mental Health Resources* is the result of the work of many people beyond the names on the front cover. The content of this book and its presentation have evolved significantly from the first edition, building on the efforts of the original team.

Throughout the revision process, dozens of mental health professionals—psychologists, counselors, clinical social workers, psychiatrists, and others—participated in vital research and interviews, providing unique perspectives and professional expertise that greatly augmented the practicality of the book. Many more reviewed and gave feedback on the manuscript before publication to help ensure it would be the most accurate and effective resource possible for Stephen Ministers. To all of them, thank you.

Thanks also to the Stephen Ministers and Stephen Leaders who enriched this book with their wisdom and experience through in-person and phone interviews, as well as through reviewing the manuscript. The insights they shared from their firsthand experience with Stephen Ministry were immensely valuable.

Finally, the assistance of many members of the Stephen Ministries staff is greatly appreciated, including the Stephen Ministries editorial and proofing teams for helping to polish the text and Kirk Geno for cover design and typesetting. A special thanks to Jana Tunell for her administrative skills and support from the first day of this project.

ABOUT THE AUTHORS

Rev. Kenneth C. Haugk, Ph.D., is a pastor, clinical psychologist, and teacher. He received his Ph.D. in clinical psychology from Washington University and his M.Div. from Concordia Seminary, both in St. Louis, Missouri. A member of the American Psychological Association, Dr. Haugk maintained a private practice as a clinical psychologist for a number of years and has taught psychology and leadership at several universities and seminaries.

Dr. Haugk is the founder and Executive Director of Stephen Ministries St. Louis. Over the years, he has written many books and courses on caring topics, such as *Christian Caregiving—a Way of Life*, *Don't Sing Songs to a Heavy Heart*, *Speaking the Truth in Love*, *Journeying through Grief*, and *Cancer—Now What?* Dr. Haugk has also published widely in psychological journals and popular periodicals.

Ken lives in St. Louis, where he enjoys playing basketball and tennis, rooting for the Cardinals, and spending time with his two daughters, son-in-law, and three grandchildren.

Isaac B. Akers is a member of the program staff at Stephen Ministries. He graduated with a bachelor of fine arts in creative writing from Truman State University in Kirksville, Missouri. He is also an Eagle Scout.

A trained Stephen Minister and Stephen Leader, Isaac joined the team at Stephen Ministries in 2015. In addition to helping research, develop, and write new resources, he also scripts and directs training videos as part of the video production team, assists in creating publicity materials, and serves at Stephen Ministry Leader's Training Courses in a variety of roles.

Originally from Des Moines, Iowa, Isaac currently resides in St. Louis, where he spends his free time taking art classes, playing soccer, and maintaining an arts and media blog.

STEPHEN MINISTRIES

Stephen Ministries is an international not-for-profit Christian educational organization founded in 1975 and based in St. Louis, Missouri. Its mission is:

> To equip the saints for the work of ministry, for building up the body of Christ, until all of us come to the unity of the faith and of the knowledge of the Son of God, to maturity, to the measure of the full stature of Christ.
> *Ephesians 4:12–13*

The 40-person staff of Stephen Ministries carries out this mission by developing and delivering high-quality, Christ-centered training and resources to:

- help congregations and other organizations equip and organize people to do meaningful ministry; and
- help individuals grow spiritually, relate and care more effectively, and live out their faith in daily life.

Best known for the Stephen Ministry system of lay caregiving, Stephen Ministries also publishes books and conducts seminars on a variety of topics, including grief, assertiveness, dealing with cancer, spiritual gifts, leadership, and crisis care.

A number of these resources are described on the following pages. To learn more about these and other resources or to order them, visit stephenministries.org or call (314) 428-2600.

Additional Resources from Stephen Ministries

Journeying through Grief

Journeying through Grief is a set of four short books that individuals, congregations, and other organizations can share with grieving people at four crucial times during the first year after a loved one has died.

Book 1: *A Time to Grieve,* sent three weeks after the loss

Book 2: *Experiencing Grief,* sent three months after the loss

Book 3: *Finding Hope and Healing,* sent six months after the loss

Book 4: *Rebuilding and Remembering,* sent eleven months after the loss

Each book focuses on the feelings and issues the person is likely to be experiencing at that point in their grief, offering reassurance, encouragement, and hope. In *Journeying through Grief,* Kenneth Haugk writes in a warm, caring style. He shares from the heart, drawing on his personal and professional experience and from the insights of many others. The books provide a simple yet powerful way to express ongoing concern to a bereaved person throughout the difficult first year.

Each set comes with four mailing envelopes and a tracking card that makes it easy to know when to send each book.

Also available is a *Giver's Guide* containing suggestions for using the books as well as sample letters that can be personalized and adapted to send with them.

Additional Resources from Stephen Ministries

Don't Sing Songs to a Heavy Heart: How to Relate to Those Who Are Suffering

Pastors, lay caregivers, and suffering people alike have high praise for *Don't Sing Songs to a Heavy Heart* by Kenneth Haugk, a warm and practical resource for what to do and say to hurting people in times of need.

Forged in the crucible of Dr. Haugk's own suffering and grief, *Don't Sing Songs to a Heavy Heart* draws from his personal experience and from extensive research with more than 4,000 other people.

For anyone who has ever felt helpless in the face of another person's pain, *Don't Sing Songs to a Heavy Heart* offers practical guidance and common-sense suggestions for how to care in ways that hurting people welcome—while avoiding the pitfalls that can add to their pain.

With its combination of sound psychology and solid biblical truths, *Don't Sing Songs to a Heavy Heart* is an excellent guide for anyone who wants to better care for those who are suffering.

Additional Resources from Stephen Ministries

Cancer—Now What?
Taking Action, Finding Hope, and Navigating the Journey Ahead

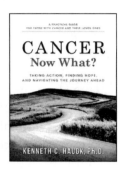

Cancer—Now What? is a book to give to people with cancer and to their loved ones, helping them navigate the medical, emotional, relational, and spiritual challenges they may encounter.

In writing the book, Kenneth Haugk drew on everything he learned as he walked alongside his wife, Joan, during her battle with cancer. He built on that foundation by conducting in-depth research with thousands of cancer survivors, loved ones of people with cancer, and medical professionals, incorporating their wisdom, experience, and expertise.

The result is a comprehensive, easy-to-read how-to resource, written in a warm, conversational style and covering a wide range of topics relevant to individuals and families dealing with cancer.

People who give the book to those affected by cancer include friends and relatives, pastors and congregations, oncologists and other physicians, cancer centers and hospitals, businesspeople and professionals of all kinds, and many others. For anyone wanting to support and encourage someone after a cancer diagnosis, giving a copy of *Cancer—Now What?* is a simple, powerful way to help.

A *Giver's Guide* is also available, which provides ideas for giving the book to those with cancer and their loved ones.